# Simula SpringerBriefs on Computing

## Volume 1

More information about this series at http://www.springer.com/series/13548

**Fragile**              **Robust**            **Anti-fragile**

Kjell Jørgen Hole

# Anti-fragile ICT Systems

Kjell Jørgen Hole
Department of Informatics
University of Bergen
Bergen
Norway

Simula SpringerBriefs on Computing
ISBN 978-3-319-30068-9          ISBN 978-3-319-30070-2    (eBook)
DOI 10.1007/978-3-319-30070-2

Library of Congress Control Number: 2016931422

Mathematics Subject Classification (2010): 68-02

Printed on acid-free paper

Springer International Publishing AG Switzerland is part of Springer Science+Business Media
(www.springer.com)

*To my wife, Winnie Busiku*

# Foreword

Dear reader,

Our aim with the series *Simula SpringerBriefs on Computing* is to provide compact introductions to selected fields of computing. Entering a new field of research can be quite demanding for graduate students, postdocs, and experienced researchers alike: the process often involves reading hundreds of papers, and the methods, results and notation styles used often vary considerably, which makes for a time-consuming and potentially frustrating experience. The briefs in this series are meant to ease the process by introducing and explaining important concepts and theories in a relatively narrow field, and by posing critical questions on the fundamentals of that field. A typical brief in this series should be around 100 pages and should be well suited as material for a research seminar in a well-defined and limited area of computing.

We have decided to publish all items in this series under the SpringerOpen framework, as this will allow authors to use the series to publish an initial version of their manuscript that could subsequently evolve into a full-scale book on a broader theme. Since the briefs are freely available online, the authors will not receive any direct income from the sales; however, remuneration is provided for every completed manuscript. Briefs are written on the basis of an invitation from a member of the editorial board. Suggestions for possible topics are most welcome and can be sent to aslak@simula.no.

January 2016

Prof. Aslak Tveito
CEO

Dr. Martin Peters
Executive Editor Mathematics
Springer Heidelberg, Germany

# Preface

As information and communications technology (ICT) becomes increasingly important to modern societies, there is a growing need to understand how to design and operate very large ICT systems. How should a huge system be designed and operated to support both high availability and rapid change? Will some of the system's stakeholders be exposed to events with intolerable impact? Is the system fragilizing a service of importance to millions of users? These are questions that need answers.

According to conventional wisdom, the opposite of a fragile system is a robust system. While stressors or perturbations can easily damage fragile systems, robust systems can withstand a great deal of pressure. This is why we write *handle with care* on a box with fragile contents and nothing on a box with robust contents. In 2012, essayist and scholar Nassim N. Taleb published his landmark book *Antifragility: Things That Gain from Disorder*, pointing out that the opposite of a fragile system is really a system that needs stressors to thrive. We would write *please mishandle* on a box with anti-fragile contents. Unlike robust systems, anti-fragile systems learn from events with negative impact how to adjust themselves and become stronger in a changing world. An example of an anti-fragile system is the human immune system, with its ability to adapt and self-repair. While Taleb's book discusses many natural and man-made systems that are anti-fragile, it says nothing about how to design and operate anti-fragile ICT systems.

## Anti-fragile ICT Systems

This book you hold in your hands or are reading on a computing device models large distributed ICT systems as complex adaptive systems to determine fundamental properties that make systems anti-fragile to different classes of events with a negative impact.[1] For example, a system can be anti-fragile to downtime or the spreading of malicious software or malware. Because there are many types of ICT systems and because each type can be anti-fragile to many classes of events, we cannot study all possible anti-fragile ICT systems. Instead, this book examines different aspects of anti-fragile systems carefully selected to show that the concept of anti-fragility offers a novel and useful approach to the design and operation of complex adaptive ICT systems.

The book first discusses rare events with a large negative impact and argues that it is, at best, very hard to predict all such events in complex adaptive ICT systems. It explains why it is necessary to limit the impact of these events to gain robustness and why learning from the remaining events with a small impact is necessary to achieve anti-fragility. Since loss of trust is an inherent and general threat to any ICT system, the book also models why it is vital for an organization operating an anti-fragile ICT system to build and maintain a strong trust relationship with its customer base. Next, the book discusses four design principles, namely, *modularity*, *weak links*, *redundancy*, and *diversity*, and one operational principle, the *fail fast* principle. While each principle by itself is well known and does not provide any new fundamental insight, collectively the five principles outline a novel way to design and operate anti-fragile ICT systems.

We apply the five principles in studies of how anti-fragile systems can (i) achieve high availability, (ii) prevent malware epidemics, and (iii) detect anomalies. Analyses of real ICT systems such as Netflix's media streaming solution, Norway's telecommunication (telecom) infrastructure, electronic government platforms, banking systems, and Numenta's anomaly detection software show that cloud computing is central to achieving all three goals. The book therefore concentrates on the design and operation of anti-fragile systems running on cloud computing platforms.

There are good reasons why the goals (i)–(iii) were selected. We study systems that are anti-fragile to downtime because prolonged outages constitute a serious problem in a world where users are increasingly dependent on ICT systems. Malware of many different types represents another serious problem affecting the security and well-being of all Internet users. Since "classical" signature-based malware detection techniques are inadequate, we study novel solutions to cope with the large negative impact of malware. Finally, to react quickly to local failures before they have time to spread, it is necessary to detect system anomalies early. This is a difficult challenge, since complex ICT systems have many interconnected entities. Consequently, we study a powerful and general learning algorithm to detect anomalies.

At the time of this writing, there are no general methods or theories on how to develop or operate anti-fragile ICT systems. The book studies select philosophical and practical aspects of anti-fragile ICT systems to gain an initial understanding

---

[1]The book should be printed in color or read on a device with a color screen because some of the figures are hard to understand when reproduced in black and white.

of them. The main message is that we should stop building fragile ICT systems of national or international importance and start building anti-fragile ICT systems. The book's contents are deeply influenced by Taleb's work on anti-fragile systems that thrive in a world dominated by large-impact, hard-to-predict, and rare events, Daniel E. Geer Jr.'s keynote speech at the Source 2008 Conference,[2] and Jeff Hawkins' still evolving theory on how the brain learns. The individual chapters are based on my own published research, basic results in complexity and network science, presentations by Neil Hunt[3] and Adrian Cockcroft[4] on Netflix's web-scale solution, and talks by Subutai Ahmad[5] and Scott Purdy[6] on Numenta's technology for anomaly detection.

## Who Should Read This Book

While this introductory book is, first and foremost, written for undergraduate students in computer science, the first half should be understandable to any technically educated individual interested in the design, development, and operation of large ICT systems. The first half introduces the concept of anti-fragility, describes the design and operational principles, and outlines how the principles can be applied to achieve anti-fragility to downtime. The book's second half is more technical and assumes that the reader has an elementary understanding of graphs. It describes how to achieve anti-fragility against malware spreading and how to detect anomalies. The whole book should be of interest to new graduate students looking for a research topic.

The book contains few abbreviations and formal definitions, background knowledge is introduced as needed, and studies of real systems help clarify concepts and insights. Each chapter is short and to the point, enabling reading in one or two sittings. Key information is repeated to make chapters easier to understand and the definitions of central abbreviations are repeated in each chapter they are used. An effort was made to reference easy-to-understand books, papers, reports, and webpages for readers wanting more background information. While the book argues that anti-fragile ICT solutions in the cloud should have a microservice architecture, it is not a textbook on cloud computing and microservices. More information on cloud computing platforms and how to implement microservices can be found in the References and on the Web.

---

[2]See geer.tinho.net/geer.sourceboston.txt.
[3]See youtube.com/watch?v=jCanhyFDopQ.
[4]See youtube.com/watch?v=dekV3Oq7pH8.
[5]See youtube.com/watch?v=nVCKjZWYavM.
[6]See youtube.com/watch?v=I5lSEHvngaI.

**Table 1** This book is partly based on articles published by the Institute of Electrical and Electronics Engineers (IEEE)

| Title | Authors | IEEE citation |
|---|---|---|
| Toward Risk Assessment of Large-Impact and Rare Events | K.J. Hole and L.-H. Netland | *Security & Privacy*, vol. 8 no. 3, 2010, pp. 21–27 |
| Building and Maintaining Trust in Internet Voting | L.H. Nestås and K.J. Hole | *Computer*, vol. 45, no. 5, 2012, pp. 74–80 |
| Management of Hidden Risks | K.J. Hole | *Computer*, vol. 46, no. 1, 2013, pp. 65–70 |
| Diversity Reduces the Impact of Malware | K.J. Hole | *Security & Privacy*, vol. 13, no. 3, 2015, pp. 48–54 |
| Towards Anti-fragility: A Malware-Halting Technique | K.J. Hole | *Security & Privacy*, vol. 13, no. 4, 2015, pp. 40–46 |
| Building Trust in E-Government Services | K.J. Hole | *Computer*, vol. 49, no. 1, 2016, pp. 66–74 |

# Acknowledgments

I am grateful to my colleagues Olav Lysne, Øyvind Ytrehus, and Håvard Raddum, as well as my students Tetiana Yarygina, Christian W. Otterstad, and Alexandre Vivmond for illuminating discussions and comments on early versions of the manuscript. A special thanks to the external expert reviewers Chief Information Security Officer Daniel E. Geer Jr. at In-Q-Tel and Vice President of Research Subutai Ahmad at Numenta. Thanks are also due to the internal expert reviewers at Simula Research Laboratory, Head of Department Ernst Gunnar Gran, Research Scientist Ahmed Elmokashi, and Senior Research Scientist Leon Moonen. The expert reviewers pointed out embarrassing mistakes, suggested much needed changes, and asked important questions leading to significant improvements of the text. Of course, I take full responsibility for all remaining mistakes and ambiguities in the book.

Some chapters are based on my own work published in the IEEE magazines *Security & Privacy* and *Computer*. I am grateful to the IEEE for allowing me to reuse material from the articles listed in Table 1. Thanks also to the articles' anonymous reviewers for the many useful comments and good suggestions that improved the presentation of the material. Finally, thanks to Lars-Helge Netland and Lars Hopland Nestås, my coauthors of the two first articles in Table 1.

Bergen, Norway                                                                  Kjell Jørgen Hole
December 2015

# Contents

# About the Author

**Kjell Jørgen Hole** lives in Norway. He holds a full-time position as a Professor in the Department of Informatics, University of Bergen (UiB) and a part-time position as the Head of the Security Department at the Simula Research Laboratory in Oslo. At the time of this writing, he is part of a joint effort between UiB and Simula to build a new cybersecurity research group.

While Kjell completed his Ph.D. in Coding Theory at UiB, he did most of his thesis work at the University of California, San Diego, where he worked at the Center for Magnetic Recording Research (CMRR). At CMRR, he was fortunate enough to join the "Wolf pack," led by the late Prof. Jack K. Wolf. Professor Wolf was an outstanding teacher, a dedicated thesis advisor, and, above all, a great human being.

Kjell was a postdoctoral researcher at IBM Almaden Research Center in Silicon Valley, where he conducted research on convolutional codes and artificial neural networks. Later, he worked on trellis coded modulation at the Norwegian University of Science and Technology. During this period, Kjell mainly published his research in *IEEE Transactions on Information Theory* and *IEEE Transactions on Communications*.

Kjell eventually switched fields from coding theory to cybersecurity because he wanted to do more applied research. His first research group in security became "infamous" in Norway for a few years because it shattered local myths about information technology systems' high degree of security and privacy. The group published articles in the IEEE magazines *Security & Privacy* and *Computer*. Kjell has continued to publish in these magazines.

Kjell enjoys teaching and working with students. Through the years he has supervised many master's and Ph.D. students. At UiB, he developed and taught courses and seminars in introductory programming, coding theory, information security, anti-fragile systems, and communication standards such as Wi-Fi and Bluetooth. He has also given many talks to Norwegian industry and written feature articles about security in Norwegian newspapers.

Together with two of his Ph.D. students, Kjell founded a security consultancy. While the consultancy was never a big financial success, the effort increased his appreciation of how difficult and time-consuming it is to build a successful company. Today, he is a board member of mCASH, a company operating a mobile payment solution in Norway.

# Part I
## The Concept of Anti-fragility

# Chapter 1
# Introduction

Modern societies cannot function without information and communications technology (ICT) systems. When ICT systems such as electronic government (e-government) systems, e-payment infrastructures, and mobile phone networks fail, users can still access alternative systems based on older technologies, but these alternatives are rapidly disappearing. E-government services are introduced on the Web to improve services to citizens and to free up the human resources needed to tackle the increasing health care requirements of aging populations. Since there will not be enough government employees to handle a large number of requests over the phone, on paper, or by personal appointment in the future, it is necessary to deploy e-government services that remain robust to undesirable incidents over time and that are available to citizens around the clock.

The robustness and availability of national e-payment infrastructures are also becoming increasingly important as countries are becoming cashless societies. If a nationwide e-payment infrastructure goes down in a cash-free society, people will not be able to pay for necessities. In Scandinavia, this is already more or less the case, since many people, especially the young, no longer carry cash. While Norwegian banks want to abolish cash altogether to reduce costs, there have been enough incidents over the last ten years causing unplanned downtime and erroneous account withdrawals to question whether the current e-payment infrastructure can provide the very high availability and long-term robustness required by a completely cash-free society.

Mobile phone networks have nearly replaced fixed-line phone systems in many countries. It is difficult to find spare parts for the old landline systems and they are expensive to maintain. Norway's largest telecom company wants all remaining fixed-phone subscribers to move to mobile subscription plans so it can dismantle the landline system altogether. Several large incidents have demonstrated how dependent the Norwegian population has become on mobile phone networks. When areas on the west coast of Norway lost power for several days because of a severe storm, the local inhabitants mainly complained about the mobile phone networks being down, illustrating that people now expect their mobile phones to work anytime and anywhere.

© The Author(s) 2016
K.J. Hole, *Anti-fragile ICT Systems*, Simula SpringerBriefs on Computing 1,
DOI 10.1007/978-3-319-30070-2_1

As traditional governmental services, cash-based payment systems, and landline phone networks are disappearing, there is a growing need for very large ICT systems with very high availability and sustained robustness to unwanted incidents. How should such systems be designed and operated to meet the increasing expectations of users in a rapidly changing world? Is a particular system design fragilizing a service of importance to millions of users? Will users be exposed to incidents with intolerable impact? *Common mode failure* is a particularly important challenge, defined as a failure in multiple parts of a system due to a single event. How do we prevent single events from propagating and taking down many parts in the same manner? This book tries to answer these questions by modeling large ICT systems as complex adaptive systems.

## 1.1  Complex Adaptive Systems

The term *complex adaptive system* denotes a man-made or natural system consisting of many entities that interact in involved ways. The entities adapt to each other and the environment to enable the system as a whole to survive events with potentially large negative impact [1–7]. ICT systems consisting of large networked computer systems and many stakeholders, including users, operators, and owners, are complex adaptive systems, as illustrated in Fig. 1.1. The complexity is due primarily to the numerous interactions between the stakeholders and the computer systems, the large amounts of communications between the networked subsystems, and the influence of changing security and privacy policies, as well as threats such as equipment failure, extreme weather, and sabotage. Collections of software services running on cloud computing platforms and nationwide infrastructures for mobile telecom constitute two particularly interesting classes of complex adaptive ICT systems with many users, mutually dependent entities, and self-regulating behaviors.

To gain an understanding of why governments and companies build complex adaptive ICT systems, we consider how valuable distributed ICT systems are to their

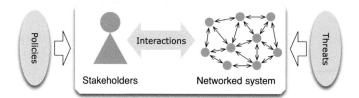

**Fig. 1.1**  A complex ICT system's global behavior is caused by dynamic interactions between the stakeholders and the networked computer system and by interactions between the network's many subsystems. Changes to policies, threats, or subsystems can cause sudden and large changes in global behavior

owners. Here, value can be the ability to provide a population with transactional services on the Web or the revenue from an online social network. Consider a system with $N$ users. The number of possible pairs of connections between users is $N(N-1)/2$, giving rise to Metcalfe's law, stating that the value of a system is proportional to the square of the number of connected users, $N^2$. Alternatively, there are $2^N - N - 1$ possible sub-groups of users, resulting in Reed's law, stating that the value of a system scales exponentially with the number of users, $2^N$. Both laws indicate that the value of distributed ICT systems grows very rapidly with the number of users, making it desirable for governments and companies to build huge ICT systems of high complexity. In addition, for many networked systems, every new user makes a system's services more valuable to the other users.

Complex adaptive systems contain *feedback loops*, as illustrated in Fig. 1.2. A feedback loop is a series of interacting processes that together result in a system adapting to the effect of its previous behavior. Feedback loops are what make complex systems adaptive. The loops create emergent global patterns or behaviors. *Positive* (escalating or compounding) feedback loops propagate and turn local events into global events, affecting whole systems, while *negative* (dampening or stabilizing) feedback loops limit the impact of local events affecting parts of systems. Negative feedback typically stabilizes a system's global behavior over a certain operating range, while positive feedback creates extreme global behavior outside the normal operating range [1, 3, 4]. Ideally, complex adaptive ICT systems should prevent positive feedback loops from ever propagating local failures into extreme global behaviors and causing systemic failures.

The emergent global behaviors of complex adaptive ICT systems are often modeled as stochastic events with given probability distributions. We distinguish between thin-tailed and thick-tailed distributions (see Chap. 2). If the tails are thin, then outliers in the form of extreme global behaviors can be ignored because the thin tails make the outliers very unlikely. When the distributions have thick tails, the outliers cannot be ignored because the probability that at least one outlier will occur is significant. Many man-made systems, including ICT systems, have positive feedback loops that cause certain local events to propagate and create extreme global behaviors. The extreme behaviors, especially unplanned downtime, become more common than stakeholders can accept. These outliers are modeled by probability distributions with thick tails. Unfortunately, classical methods for risk analysis based on predictions of

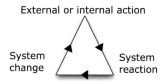

**Fig. 1.2** Generic feedback loop: an external or internal action leads to a system reaction. The reaction then causes the system to change, which initiates another action and the process repeats

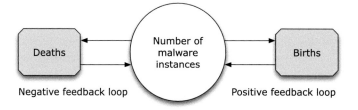

**Fig. 1.3** Birth–death process illustrating malware spreading

future events tend to underestimate or ignore extreme global behaviors in complex adaptive ICT systems, even though these events may very well dominate the overall risk to stakeholders.

A vulnerability in a man-made system can be a flaw in the design, a bug in the implementation, or a mistake in the system's operation or management. Any complex man-made system has vulnerabilities. Coincidental errors and malfunctions, as well as hostile and targeted attacks, exploit vulnerabilities to cause failures leading to extreme global behavior such as unplanned system downtime. In particular, malicious software, or *malware*, can exploit vulnerabilities and cause information leakage. Figure 1.3 depicts a simple model of an infectious malware epidemic that involves a positive feedback loop of increased births and a negative loop of increased deaths. Without deaths, the population size will increase exponentially, that is, negative feedback is needed to keep the positive feedback under control [1].

The observed fragility of complex ICT systems to prolonged downtime and malware infections demonstrates the need for better system design, implementation, operation, and management. The many interactions between the adaptive entities in the systems create a highly non-linear and time-varying relation between the input and output that makes it nearly impossible to predict extreme global behavior. Hence, we need non-predictable techniques to create complex adaptive ICT systems. Taleb's work [8–12] suggests that we should develop and operate so-called *anti-fragile* systems characterized by two important properties: First, an anti-fragile ICT system fails early with a small, local impact to break positive feedback loops before they can create extreme global behaviors. Second, the prevention of extreme global behaviors allows stakeholders to learn from small-impact incidents about new vulnerabilities caused by changes in the system and its environment. The vulnerabilities can then be mitigated to avoid future extreme behaviors.

This book investigates how to develop and operate anti-fragile ICT systems. Cloud-based systems are emphasized because cloud computing platforms utilizing virtualization technologies greatly facilitate the creation and maintenance of anti-fragility compared to traditional datacenters without virtualization technologies (see Chap. 5).

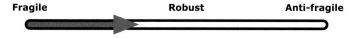

**Fig. 1.4** Toward anti-fragility

## 1.2   Fragile, Robust, and Anti-fragile Systems

The research literature has long categorized complex adaptive systems as fragile or robust to incidents with a particular type of impact. Fragile systems are vulnerable to the impacts of these incidents, while robust systems withstand or absorb them. Unlike robust systems, anti-fragile systems learn from such incidents how to function increasingly well in a changing environment [9, 10]. In fact, anti-fragile systems need incidents to remain well adapted to their environments. Without the ability to learn from incidents, anti-fragile systems become fragile over time as the systems themselves and their environments change. The human immune system, with its ability to adapt and self-repair, is a prime example of a system that is anti-fragile to many types of impact.

As depicted in Fig. 1.4, the fragility, robustness, and anti-fragility to a particular type of impact are best viewed as degrees on a spectrum with fragile systems to the left, robust systems in the middle, and anti-fragile systems to the right. Systems have to become robust before they can become anti-fragile and no system can be anti-fragile to all possible types of impact [10]. At present, there is no general technique to measure fragility, robustness, and anti-fragility. However, this book will demonstrate that it is not difficult to recognize when a system is fragile, for example, to downtime or malware spreading. Furthermore, it will introduce design and operational principles that move toward anti-fragility in Fig. 1.4.

## 1.3   Overview of Book

Taleb [10] introduced the concept of anti-fragility to analyze and explain why it is not enough for large natural or man-made systems to be robust to predictable events with large impact. In an unpredictable world, systems must be able to handle randomness, volatility, and unforeseen large-impact events. Learning from incidents is needed to prevent systems from developing fragilities over time.

So far there are no general methods or theories on how to develop or operate anti-fragile ICT systems. This book studies select philosophical and practical aspects of anti-fragile ICT systems to gain an initial understanding of them. The main message is that we should stop building fragile ICT systems of national or international importance and start building anti-fragile ICT systems.

The book is divided into five parts. Part I discusses the concept of anti-fragility, why the concept is important, and how to achieve anti-fragility in general. Part II outlines in some detail how different ICT systems can achieve anti-fragility to down-time and Part III develops a technique to achieve anti-fragility to malware spreading. Since we need to detect failures to achieve anti-fragility, Part IV discusses how to detect anomalies in system behavior. Finally, Part V summarizes the book's main insights and suggests potential venues for further work.

The contents of Parts I and II should be easy to understand for most readers, while an additional effort may be needed to understand the more complicated content of Parts III and IV. To facilitate understanding, certain chapters repeat central information introduced earlier in the book. The following sections provide more detailed summaries of the five parts.

## 1.4  Creating and Maintaining Anti-fragility

Part I, including the current chapter, outlines how to create and operate complex adaptive ICT systems with anti-fragility to different types of impact, such as unplanned downtime and malware spreading. Chapter 2 first discusses rare events with a large negative impact and argues that it is, at best, very hard to predict all such events in complex systems. Next, it explains why a system must limit the impact of these events to gain robustness and why learning from the remaining events with a small impact is necessary to achieve anti-fragility.

While organizations with anti-fragile systems must accept and learn from failures, they also need to focus on building trust with users to maintain and increase their user base. Chapter 3 defines a simple agent-based model of how trust changes in a user population. The model illustrates that trust is fragile to incidents directly affecting few users and that massive distrust is robust to large efforts to regain trust. Since it is very hard to predict which events have the potential to create massive distrust, organizations must have procedures in place to handle the impact of incidents before distrust starts to spread.

The design of an ICT system is the process of defining its components, interfaces, data formats, data flow, and data storage that together satisfy specified availability, performance, and scalability requirements. Chapter 4 first provides four design principles that isolate local failures, keeping their impacts small, while supporting stringent requirements. Second, it introduces one operational principle that enables stakeholders to quickly learn from natural and induced failures to maintain a level of anti-fragility as a system and its environment change. While each principle alone does not provide any new fundamental insight, collectively the five principles outline a novel way to design and operate anti-fragile ICT systems. In particular, it is possible to create ICT systems with higher availability than today's tightly connected and highly optimized systems with limited redundancy and diversity.

## 1.5 Anti-fragility to Downtime

A cloud computing platform enables ubiquitous, convenient, on-demand access to a shared pool of configurable computing resources such as CPUs, networks, memory, and databases that can be rapidly provisioned and released with minimal management effort or service provider interaction [13, 14]. Virtualization technologies are used to abstract the resources for applications and end users. The availability of a cloud-based ICT system is measured by the percentage of time it is accessible to users. A high availability of 99.99 %, referred to as four nines of availability, corresponds to about 53 min of downtime each year. A complex ICT system is fragile to downtime if its availability is unacceptably low to some stakeholders, robust if the availability is acceptable to all stakeholders, and anti-fragile if stakeholders or the technical system itself learn to maintain an acceptable availability as the system and its environment change.

Part II discusses how the five design and operational principles from Chap. 4 can be implemented on cloud computing platforms to create highly available software solutions and mobile telecom infrastructures. To gain insight, we reason about real systems using philosophical concepts, objects, figures, and impressions of past incidents. The thinking is based solely on publicly available information and is rooted in complexity science [15–20], where whole systems cannot be understood by exclusively studying their parts; instead, it is necessary to emphasize interrelationships and changes to understand the systems' dynamic global behaviors.

Chapter 5 outlines how Netflix implemented the five principles in their cloud-based web-scale solution for media streaming. Chapter 6 explains why Norway's e-government system has experienced too much downtime and describes how a new cloud-based system founded on the five principles can achieve anti-fragility to downtime. The chapter also references the UK e-government system to argue the need for user-focused and iterative software development to achieve anti-fragility. Finally, Chap. 7 discusses fragility to downtime in Norwegian telecom systems and outlines how the five principles applied on cloud computing platforms can make telecom systems anti-fragile to downtime.

## 1.6 Anti-fragility to Malware Spreading

Malware is any form of malicious software used to disrupt computer operations, gather sensitive information, or gain unauthorized access to private computer systems. Malware appears as executable code, scripts, active content, and other software. Malware includes computer viruses, worms, trojans, ransomware, spyware, scareware, and other types of malicious programs. Worldwide, trojans, worms, and viruses continue to dominate among the many malware types.

Malware is a serious threat to anybody using a computer system connected to the Internet [21, 22]. A networked system is fragile to malware spreading when local outbreaks spread far and robust when new malware outbreaks have very limited spreading. The system is anti-fragile to malware spreading if it first learns to reduce the fraction of infected devices, for example, to less than 1 % and then manages to keep the fraction of infected devices low even as the spreading mechanism of the malware changes.

Part III develops a novel malware-halting technique that prevents frequent malware outbreaks from propagating over huge networks of computing devices. Calculations and simulations using slightly modified epidemiological models from network science [23] determine the time-averaged fraction of infected devices. Chapter 8 outlines how application stores utilizing compilers with so-called diversity engines [24] can generate enough software diversity to gain robustness to malware spreading by halting frequent malware outbreaks with a fixed spreading mechanism. It also argues that diversity slows down persistent targeted attacks.

Chapter 9 studies malware types that spread over networks with an unknown topology. The malware studied have the ability to reinfect nodes multiple times. Acquaintance immunization [25] and software diversity are combined to gain robustness to malware reinfections. While reinfections generally help malware stay alive for a long time, the described halting technique prevents malware outbreaks from spreading very far before they die out.

Chapter 10 combines cloud computing, time-varying software diversity, immunization, and imperfect malware detection/removal to model and analyze networks that gain anti-fragility to malware spreading by learning to halt and remove malware with unknown and time-varying spreading mechanisms. Non-infectious malware mistakenly downloaded by computer users are viewed as infectious malware with limited spreading ability.

## 1.7  Anomaly Detection

To achieve anti-fragility to a particular type of intolerable impact, local failures must be detected before they can propagate into systemic failures. Humans are often needed to determine whether a local anomaly is just a benign change or a local failure with the potential to create a systemic failure. Current ICT systems deploy various techniques and heuristics to detect anomalies. For example, banks and credit card companies have a rich set of heuristics to detect fraud [26].

In Part IV, we study a general learning algorithm based on the biology of the brain's neocortex. The learning algorithm was developed by Hawkins [27] and implemented in software by the company Numenta (http://numenta.com). The algorithm is able to predict the behavior of a wide variety of systems. If a prediction and the actual behavior differ, then an anomaly is detected. Chapter 11 discusses the biological basis for the learning algorithm and provides an overview of the algorithm itself.

Numenta's experiments with different types of streaming data, including metric data from cloud applications, show that the algorithm detects anomalies that are hard for humans to discover. Chapter 12 illustrates how the early detection of subtle anomalies allows systems or their stakeholders to take early action to prevent local failures from creating intolerable impact.


## 1.8 Ongoing Explanatory Work

Part V consists of Chap. 13. It summarizes the book's main insights and discusses possible research directions to further increase the understanding of anti-fragile ICT systems.

Overall, this book is a result of the author's ongoing long-term effort to understand what Taleb's [8–12] philosophical investigations and Geer's [28–33] systems thinking tell us about the design, implementation, operation, and management of complex adaptive ICT systems. Both Geer and Taleb look to nature to understand anti-fragile systems. In nature, sexual reproduction creates many species consisting of individuals who genetically differ from each other. An infectious disease is very unlikely to wipe out an entire population, since some individuals are almost certainly genetically immune. In other words, while each individual is vulnerable to diseases, the population survives due to a diverse gene pool.

While the author avoids superficial references to biology and Darwin's theory of evolution in the book, he agrees with Geer and Taleb that there is much to learn from nature on how to build complex ICT systems. In particular, Geer has stated several times that computing devices should have a relatively short life unless they are easy to upgrade. This observation has strongly influenced the work in Part III, leading to a novel approach to malware halting.

It is hard to precisely model the global behaviors of complex ICT systems. Rather than trying to develop sophisticated models to accurately simulate the behaviors of real systems, this book develops toy models to gain an understanding of them. While these models cannot predict the global behavior of real systems, they provide explanations of important system properties. The suggested malware-halting technique in Part III demonstrates that it is possible to create novel approaches and solutions to difficult problems by developing simple agent-based models of networked ICT systems and then employing techniques from network science to analyze the models' properties.

Since many of the ideas presented in this book have yet to be tested in real systems and since the book by no means covers all aspects of anti-fragile ICT systems, the author welcomes criticism and debate to shed further light on how to develop and operate anti-fragile ICT systems. Understanding all aspects of these systems is an important task for both the research community and the industry—not only for the author.

# Chapter 2
# Achieving Anti-fragility

A stakeholder is a person or institution with a legitimate interest in a given information and communications technology (ICT) system. Examples of stakeholders are users, owners, operators, regulatory government agencies, system architects, and software developers. Given a set of stakeholders, a complex adaptive ICT system is *fragile* to a particular type of negative impact, for example, downtime, if a possible large impact is unacceptable to some stakeholders in the set and *robust* if all possible impacts are acceptable to all stakeholders. The ICT system is *anti-fragile* if it learns (perhaps with help from some stakeholders) to maintain an acceptable impact to all stakeholders as the system and environment change over time.

This chapter first considers rare failures causing unacceptable impact and argues that it is very hard to predict all such future events. Second, it argues that it is necessary to limit the impact of failures to gain robustness and to learn from the remaining small failures to achieve anti-fragility. Third, the chapter discusses limitations of classical risk analysis methods before finally introducing an alternative definition of risk in complex adaptive ICT systems.

## 2.1 Black and Gray Swans

As stated in Chap. 1, global emergent behaviors of complex adaptive systems are modeled as stochastic events with given probability distributions. For simplicity, we assume that the studied behavior of a system is modeled by a continuous random variable with a distribution given by a probability density function (PDF). Figure 2.1 shows two PDFs, each with a left and right tail. The tails determine the probability of outliers in the form of extreme global behavior. The left tail defines the probabilities of outliers with huge negative impact, while the right tail defines the probabilities of outliers with huge positive impact. We are only concerned with negative impact in this book.

As illustrated in Fig. 2.1, there are PDFs with thin tails and thick (or fat) tails. If a PDF has thin tails, then most events occur close to the mean of the PDF. Furthermore,

© The Author(s) 2016
K.J. Hole, *Anti-fragile ICT Systems*, Simula SpringerBriefs on Computing 1,
DOI 10.1007/978-3-319-30070-2_2

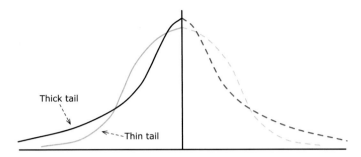

**Fig. 2.1** Two PDFs, one with *thin tails* and one with *thick tails*

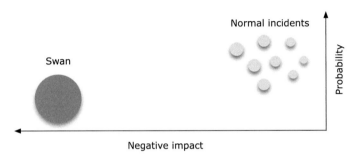

**Fig. 2.2** Probability and negative impact of a single nonrecurrent swan incident versus recurrent incidents. The swan is an outlier

outliers far from the mean have such low probabilities that they can be ignored for all practical purposes. This is the case for the thin-tailed bell curve (or normal distribution). However, if a PDF has thick tails, then the probabilities of the outliers are too large to be ignored. Observe that a PDF can also have one thick tail and one thin tail.

Large man-made systems designed in a top-down manner by successively being broken down into smaller parts tend to have global behaviors whose probabilities are defined by PDFs with thick left tails. In general, the thick tails are due to positive feedback loops created by a series of interacting processes that together result in systems adapting to the effect of their previous behaviors (see Fig. 1.2). Positive feedback loops allow for outliers with unacceptable impact [3, 4]. Taleb [9] distinguishes between two types of outliers with negative impact, namely, *black* and *gray swans*. Figure 2.2 depicts the differences in probability and impact between a nonrecurrent black or gray swan and so-called normal, recurrent incidents: Both types of swans are surprising outliers, falsifying previous assumptions about the negative impact of incidents made by most or all stakeholders of a system.

Assume an arbitrary but fixed set of stakeholders. A black swan is a metaphor for rare global behavior of a complex adaptive system whose huge negative impact comes as a total surprise to all stakeholders in the set. This type of extreme emergent behavior is the "unknown unknown," a rare bombshell event that none of the stakeholders have considered.

Two important observations can be made about black swans. First, a black swan cannot be described by any of the stakeholders because the event is completely unknown to all of them. Second, while a black swan is a total surprise to all the stakeholders considered, there may be other individuals outside the group of stakeholders for which the event is not a big surprise. As an example, while the economic crisis of 2007/2008 came as a huge surprise to most people, a few individuals, including Taleb [9], foresaw the crisis, even though they could not say when the crisis would occur or exactly how serious the consequences would be.

A gray swan is a metaphor for rare global behavior with a large negative impact that is somewhat predictable but typically overlooked by most of the stakeholders considered. It is the "known unknown," a rare event that some know is possible but no one knows when or whether it will occur. Because a gray swan is not a complete surprise to all stakeholders, it tends to have less impact than a black swan. However, its impact is still huge. For simplicity, we often neglect to define a set of stakeholders when we discuss gray and black swans. However, the reader should assume that users, owners, software developers, operators, and regulatory government agencies are always among the stakeholders.

## 2.2 Examples of Swans

Hindsight bias, or the knew-it-all-along effect, is the natural tendency, after an incident has occurred, to conclude that the incident was foreseeable, despite there having been little or no objective basis for this conclusion. Hindsight bias [6, 9] causes observers to miscategorize black swans as gray swans after the fact. Moreover, differences in understanding, personal involvement, and available information cause individuals to disagree on whether a large-impact event is a black or gray swan at all. Consequently, it is hard to make all observers agree on what incidents are gray and black swans in complex ICT systems, especially when the observers have no access to the stakeholders. We can, however, give examples of incidents that many, but perhaps not all, security experts will categorize as swans.

When the computer worm Nimda first appeared on the Internet in September 2001, it spread quickly, causing hundreds of millions of dollars in damages, according to press reports. Although the public was familiar with worms at the time, we characterize Nimda as a black swan because it was the first infectious malware with multiple attack methods [30]. Nimda's five attack methods made it extremely difficult to foresee all of their consequences. The large number of infected computers demonstrates that the attacks surprised computer owners, software vendors, and information technology departments. While NIMDA caused much damage, it could have been much worse. The worm occurred only one week after the 9/11 terrorist attacks. According to Geer [30], the backdoor installed by NIMDA could have been exploited to run denial-of-service attacks on emergency services all over the United States, causing public loss of confidence after the nationwide uncertainty created by the shock of 9/11.

In August 2001, a company providing services to Norwegian banks installed new disks in a backup system used to mirror the production environment. System operators inadvertently routed the instruction to format the disks to the production environment rather than to the backup system. The error rendered production data inaccessible on about 280 disks, thus halting the production environment. This rare incident affected 114 banks and roughly 1 million users. It took seven days before payment card, ATM, Internet banking, and phone banking services were all back to normal operation. While the total cost to the company is not publicly known, it was likely very large, since the company had to compensate the banks for their financial losses. This gray swan occurred because administrators did not pay enough attention to the established security procedures and thus triggered a single point of failure in the system.

While we should always try to remove single points of failures from ICT systems, there exist systems for which a single point of failure is an essential side effect of the design [30]. The single red phone on the American president's desk is a good example. Many red phones would be a far worse solution from a risk management point of view. When a single point of failure is a design requirement, we need to deploy defense in depth, which is not a research-grade problem. Hence, we will not discuss single points of failure in any detail in this book.

## 2.3   Limiting the Impact of Failures

To understand the challenges of curbing the impact of failures in complex ICT systems, we study why it is so hard to predict rare events with large negative impacts [9, 34]. Let the term *incident* denote an event with negative impact. To predict any future incident, we must describe the incident, estimate its probability, and calculate the impact. Many incidents causing, for example, unplanned downtime are predictable, especially incidents due to single points of failure. As an example, ICT systems without redundant data storage or backup power are sure to fail sooner or later. However, swan incidents exist that are very hard or even impossible to predict.

In fact, it is very hard to accurately predict extreme global behavior in complex ICT systems [7, 34]. Because the systems have too many dynamic interactions for humans to even enumerate all the possible scenarios leading to outliers with a huge negative impact, it is easy for all stakeholders to overlook a future swan, thus making it black. Furthermore, it is hard to estimate the probabilities of identified gray swans, because a complex system changes significantly and perhaps abruptly over time and because a system's recorded history might not contain a single swan; for example, a 100-year flood is not likely to show up in 10 years of historical data.

Complex systems' lack of well-defined boundaries makes it hard to build models to accurately estimate the probabilities of gray swans. Taleb utilizes power laws to illustrate that small model errors greatly affect rare events' estimated probabilities

[11]. Experience with a particular system type helps estimate gray swan probabilities in a similar new system. However, because the estimation of gray swan probabilities in a large system requires many assumptions, especially when considering the design of a system that has not yet been implemented, the estimates carry significant uncertainty. All in all, it is very hard for stakeholders to accurately predict the gray swans that actually occur. In addition, even if a system owner mitigates all the gray swans, an unknown black swan can still cause huge damage.

Since the probability of each black and gray swan is both small and unknown, it is tempting to ignore swans altogether. However, because a complex ICT system is typically vulnerable to many swans, there is a significant probability that at least one swan will occur. Thus, no matter the quality of the risk analysis, swans causing unacceptable impact will occur in complex ICT systems sooner or later; unless the systems are especially designed and operated to limit the impact of rare, unforeseeable events [3, 4, 6, 10].

To avoid surprising outliers and help ensure event distributions with thin left tails, Chap. 4 proposes four design principles to isolate local failures affecting small parts of systems, thus preventing them from propagating into systemic or global failures affecting complete systems.

## 2.4   Learning from Small Failures

In an interesting monograph, Sidney Dekker [17] recounts series of small, rather insignificant everyday decisions leading to major disasters, including large oil spills and plane crashes. There are no easily detectable properties of the decisions that signal major disasters in the future. In fact, given the information available at the time, most of the decisions are reasonable when studied in isolation. However, over time, the decisions reduced the diversity and redundancy of the systems and made them steadily more fragile to disasters. This fragilizing process was mainly driven by pressure to use fewer resources and to produce results faster. Some stakeholders contributed to the system fragility by introducing conflicting requirements and regulations, while other stakeholders encouraged risky behavior to reach certain goals, such as producing large quantities of oil.

The accident scenarios described by Dekker [17] further demonstrate that broken parts are not the major reason for disasters in complex adaptive systems. Rather, it is the stakeholders' inability to cope with the complexity of a system and its changing environment. Lack of understanding, insufficient communication between stakeholders, and pressure to improve a system's "efficiency" all increase its fragility to disasters. Dekker shows how stakeholders build and operate systems they do not fully understand. While stakeholders grasp the functionality of each part, the huge amount of interactions between the many parts and the changing rules and regulations governing the operations of the systems make it impossible for stakeholders to prevent rare catastrophic events.

In summary, man-made complex systems in general and complex ICT systems in particular tend to drift into systemic failure because they become increasingly fragile due to internal and external changes. The drift occurs slowly, with few or no obvious indications of increased fragility before a major incident occurs [2, 17, 35]. Since black and gray swans in complex systems limit the stakeholders' ability to predict extreme global behavior with a huge negative impact, the stakeholders must analyze local failures (with limited impact) and introduce countermeasures to avoid increased fragility due to local failures propagating into global failures. Daniel Kahneman's pioneering work [36] and a monograph by Michael T. Nygard [35] confirm the discussed limits of prediction and the need to learn from local failures. Since the capacity to detect small failures is crucial to determine vulnerabilities, the comprehensive monitoring of a system's behavior is extremely important to achieve anti-fragility. The goal is not to prevent all failures in an ICT system but to avoid silent failures and quickly start necessary repairs.

Because systemic failures are most often, but not always, initiated by local failures that propagate due to positive feedback loops, it is possible to prevent many swans by detecting local failures and preventing them from propagating. While all swans may not be absolutely prevented, it is possible to make rare events rarer and reduce their impact. Chapter 4 proposes an operational principle that induces artificial failures into a system to quickly detect vulnerabilities with the potential to cause systemic failures. A team of experts with diverse skill sets should learn from the induced incidents because a team could respond faster and gain more insights than a single individual. All team members should have "skin in the game" [10, Chap. 23]: When the members face the consequences of their actions and suffer failure as well as enjoy success, they become motivated to learn rapidly and not take unwarranted chances. A team of software developers has skin in the game when it is responsible for both the development and operations (DevOps) of its software [37, 38]. Another way of introducing skin in the game is to let team members use their own software as much as possible.

The increasingly popular DevOps methodology emphasizes communication, collaboration, and integration between software developers and information technology operations professionals. DevOps is a response to the interdependence of software development and information technology operations. It facilitates learning from natural and induced failures and encourages software developers to create robust code so they do not have to fix problems at three o'clock in the morning.

## 2.5  An Alternative Justification

We have argued that a complex ICT system exposed to swan incidents must be anti-fragile to the swans' impacts to thrive over time. According to Taleb [10], the need for anti-fragility can be summarized as follows: Let $X$ be a random variable representing events with some probability distribution (given by a PDF) and let $h(X)$ be another random variable representing the possible impacts, for example, the financial costs to a stakeholder. In practice, we care about $h(X)$ and not $X$. While it is often hard to change the thick-tail distribution of $X$, it can be much easier to change the distribution of $h(X)$. Our goal is to ensure that the distribution of $h(X)$ has a thin left tail to avoid intolerable costly outliers (see Fig. 2.2).

Since a complex adaptive system and its environment change over time, perhaps abruptly, the distribution of $h(X)$ also changes. The left tail of the changing distribution of $h(X)$ is unknown because we do not have sufficient data, that is, the history of the system may not contain any outliers and, even if it did, there is no guarantee that the future of the system will be anything like its past. Hence, an anti-fragile system must prevent local failures from propagating into systemic failures and use local failures to detect and remove vulnerabilities that can lead to systemic failures in the future.

While the discussed approach leads to a thinning of the left tail of $h(X)$, there is no absolute guarantee that a swan will not occur in a complex ICT system. Guaranteed swan-free ICT systems can only be achieved by keeping the systems relatively small to limit their importance and possible negative impact. It may also be necessary to isolate systems from each other, for example, systems with particularly sensitive information should not be connected to the Internet.


## 2.6   Risk Analyses Ignore Swans

The reader may wonder how classical methods for the risk analysis of ICT systems rate the impact of swans. The short answer is that they mostly ignore swans altogether. This unfortunate tendency partly explains why we continue building ICT systems with tightly interconnected parts, little diversity, and low redundancy that allow local failures to propagate into systemic failures.

Traditionally, analysts evaluate risk by estimating the probability of a threat exploiting a vulnerability and by determining the resulting incident's negative impact. Analysts often use the values low, medium, and high to approximate the probability and impact, resulting in the five-level risk matrix in Fig. 2.3. The matrix incorrectly classifies a gray swan as a medium risk because it has a low probability and high impact according to the approximations.

As an example, a nationwide outage in a power grid is a medium risk despite the outage's ability to inflict damage in the billions of dollars. Since swans, with their huge impacts, tend to dominate the total risk of complex ICT systems, the use of risk matrices has lead to a gross underestimation of the total risk associated with many systems.

The underlying problem is that risk matrices of the type depicted in Fig. 2.3 implicitly assume that the distribution of the impact $h(X)$ has a thin left tail. Since the probabilities of nonrecurrent outliers or swans are assumed to be so small that the incidents can be ignored, the risk matrix only represents recurrent incidents with larger probabilities and smaller impacts than those of swans. However, a complex adaptive ICT system with many tightly connected parts is very likely to have a $h(X)$

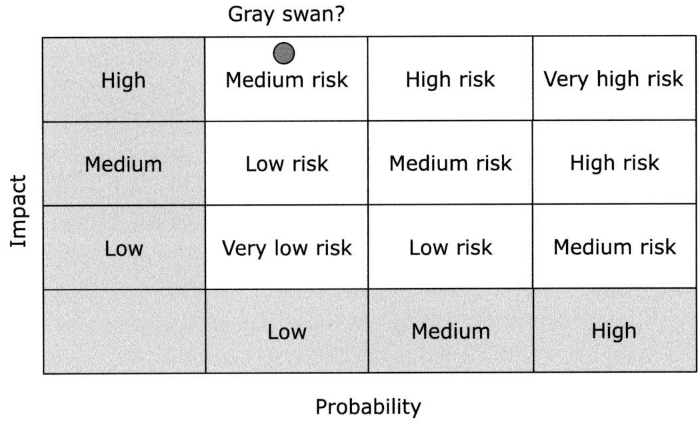

Fig. 2.3  The five-level risk matrix underestimates the risk of *gray* swans

distribution with a thick left tail, making it dangerous to use the risk matrix in Fig. 2.3 because it excludes the possibility of swans.

## 2.7  Understanding and Reducing Risk

An interesting video exists (https://www.youtube.com/watch?v=MKcZtvwch1w) of the late Peter L. Bernstein discussing risk. According to Bernstein, we talk about risk when we do not know what will happen. Risk simply means that more things can happen than will happen. Since this book focuses on swans incidents, we use a more specific and narrow definition of risk. Consider a group of one or more stakeholders with interests in a complex adaptive ICT system. We define the *risk* associated with the group of stakeholders as the largest negative impact of all incidents that can happen to the group during a fixed period. How the impact is actually measured depends on the system and the interests of the stakeholders. Impact is commonly measured in terms of financial loss. Note that our definition of risk is not based on the probability of an incident. Because the definition of risk is tailored to the book's focus on intolerable incidents, it may not be the best choice in other settings.

Risk is a consequence of dependence [31]. A part (or system) $\mathcal{X}$ *depends* on another part (system) $\mathcal{Y}$ if a failure in $\mathcal{Y}$ negatively affects the functionality of $\mathcal{X}$. The main sources of risk in an ICT system are the dependencies between its parts creating positive feedback loops, which again cause local failures to propagate into global failures. In general, the growing number of dependencies in increasingly complex systems causes incidents impacting stakeholders to become less frequent, because the systems become better at handling recurrent incidents over the normal operating range. However, at the same time, the impacts of nonrecurrent incidents are increasing due to the positive feedback loops propagating (combinations of) rare local events outside the normal operating range.

In Taleb's [9] terminology, while incidents affecting stakeholders are becoming less frequent, gray and black swans occur more often in ICT systems with tight internal integration as their complexity grows. Since it is hard to determine all the dependencies of complex systems, the probability of swans in complex ICT systems is underestimated, causing intolerable impacts because most stakeholders are not prepared for swans.

As the risk of recurrent incidents is reduced and the intervals between incidents grow longer, the assumption that complex ICT systems are "safe" also grows, thus causing a situation (actually a feedback loop) in which stakeholders create increasingly more complex systems with tightly integrated parts [31]. To counter this development and reduce the risks to the stakeholders, it is necessary to create ICT systems with only tolerable failures. Since the causes of swans are, at best, hard to predict, it is necessary to limit the impact of incidents, even though we have no a priori knowledge of their causes.

## 2.8 Taleb's Four Quadrants

Following Taleb [11, 12], we create a map to classify the negative impact of different failures in complex adaptive ICT systems. We again represent the impact of events in a complex adaptive ICT system by a continuous random variable with a particular PDF. Furthermore, we discriminate between two types of negative impacts, namely, local and global impacts. Some systems only permit the local impact of failures, while other systems allow local failures to propagate and create a global (systemic) impact. The PDF of the local or global impact has a thin or thick left tail.

The four quadrants of the map in Fig. 2.4 represent the four possible combinations of local and global impacts and thin and thick tails. The quadrants represent four classes of complex ICT systems with very different extreme behaviors. The map shows where classical risk analysis works well and where it is of questionable use

|  | Only local impact | Global impact |
|---|---|---|
| **Thin left tail** | First quadrant:<br>*Only limited local impact* | Second quadrant:<br>*Global failure possible,<br>but tolerable impact* |
| **Thick left tail** | Third quadrant:<br>*Large local impact, rigorous<br>risk management needed* | Fourth quadrant:<br>*Intolerable global impact is<br>inevitable in the long run* |

**Fig. 2.4** The impact of a failure in a complex adaptive ICT system falls within one of Taleb's four quadrants. The fourth quadrant must be avoided because it leads to intolerable systemic failures

and can lead to the gross underestimation of the risk by ignoring swans in the form of rare outliers with an intolerable negative impact.

A system in the first quadrant in Fig. 2.4 is very safe. It only experiences local failures with limited impact because the PDF of the local impact has a thin left tail. Unfortunately, it seems that today's complex ICT systems are not in this quadrant. The second quadrant is also a fairly safe place for a system. Global failures may occur, but the global impact is tolerable due to the thin left tail of the PDF. Systems in the third quadrant only experience local failures, but these can have a relatively large impact because the PDF of the local impact has a thick left tail. Hence, rigorous risk management is needed.

Systems in the fourth quadrant must be avoided because they are vulnerable to gray and black swans with an intolerable impact. While the probability of a single swan is small, ICT systems in the fourth quadrant are usually vulnerable to many swans, making it inevitable that one will occur sooner or later. As explained in Sects. 2.3 and 2.6, classical risk analysis cannot handle nonrecurrent swans in the fourth quadrant.

We want to develop and operate complex adaptive ICT systems where all failures are local with limited impact, that is, we want the systems to fall in the first quadrant in Fig. 2.4. However, since we will not succeed in limiting absolutely all failures of complex national and international ICT infrastructures, these systems will more likely end up in the second or third quadrant, which is also acceptable as long as we avoid swans with an intolerable impact in the fourth quadrant.

## 2.9  Discussion and Summary

If we consider a complex adaptive ICT system over a period of, say, 20 years, then normal incidents will occur repeatedly during the period. Hence, these recurrent incidents should become less and less surprising to the system's stakeholders. The same is not true for gray and black swans. Because swans are so rare, they will not occur multiple times over the considered period. Consequently, swans are, at best, very hard to predict, since there is little or nothing in the system's history to signal their future occurrence. However, since complex ICT systems are vulnerable to many swans, the probability that at least one swan will occur is too large to be ignored.

Given a set of stakeholders, a complex ICT system is fragile to a particular type of negative impact if a possible large impact is unacceptable to some stakeholders in the set and robust if all possible impacts are acceptable to all stakeholders. It is not enough for complex ICT systems to be robust, because internal and external changes fragilize complex systems over time, making them increasingly vulnerable to large-impact events, including swans. Since we cannot hope to predict all negative events that can significantly impact complex ICT systems, we must build systems that limit the impact of incidents of unknown origin and learn from events with a small negative impact how to limit the impact of all incidents. The resulting ICT systems are anti-fragile when they manage to reduce and maintain acceptable impacts to all stakeholders.

Stochastic modeling is much used in many research areas, particularly in modern financial theory. Financial models are very often based on PDFs with thin tails, leading to a gross underestimation of the risks associated with the economic processes being modeled. To better understand the devastating consequences of using the wrong stochastic models, the reader should consult the books of Pablo Triana [39] and Benoit Mandelbrot and Richard Hudson [40]. Both argue that standard financial models have led investors to take on huge hidden risks with ruinous consequences. Together, Taleb [8–11], Triana, Mandelbrot, and Hudson illustrate the folly of trying to predict extreme global behavior in complex adaptive systems of global importance.

# Chapter 3
# The Need to Build Trust

An organization operating and managing a complex adaptive information and communications technology (ICT) system is said to be anti-fragile when, over time, the organization is able to protect the user population from serious consequences of system failures and simultaneously provide digital services fulfilling the users' changing needs [41]. According to Chap. 2, failures are inevitable in a complex ICT system. Unless a user population has a high level of trust in the system, the population may abandon the system after a failure. Hence, any anti-fragile organization running a complex ICT system must maintain a high level of trust over time to keep their users after inevitable system failures.

To better understand why it is critical for any anti-fragile organization to maintain user trust, this chapter first defines the concept of trust and then develops a model of a user population whose individuals influence each others' levels of trust in an ICT system, for example, an e-government platform with digital services. The model demonstrates that a population's trust decreases rapidly when distrust within small groups of individuals starts to spread. Further, it illustrates why it is hard to determine which incidents will lead to widespread distrust and clarifies why it is very difficult to create pervasive trust when there is much distrust. We find that a population's trust is fragile to incidents directly affecting a few individuals while widespread distrust is robust against concentrated efforts to rebuild trust. Finally, the chapter discusses approaches to limit the spread of distrust and maintain a high level of trust.

## 3.1 Defining Trust

Trust can be viewed as a computational construct whose value depends on the context. The value is likely to change over time. Here, an individual's trust in an entity is specified by three concepts: *trust*, *mistrust*, and *distrust*, viewed as mutually exclusive states representing different degrees of trust. Mistrust represents a general sense of unease toward an ICT system based on mostly unverified information, while users

© The Author(s) 2016
K.J. Hole, *Anti-fragile ICT Systems*, Simula SpringerBriefs on Computing 1,
DOI 10.1007/978-3-319-30070-2_3

distrust a system because of negative experiences or reliable information from experts about serious problems with the system. As an example, users distrust an Internet banking system after suffering financial losses, but they only mistrust the system after being told about security problems by family, friends, or co-workers.

Since most users do not fully understand how an ICT system operates or why incidents occur, they will seek advice from others about what to believe about the system; that is, their levels of trust are influenced by other stakeholders. Mistrust is a less stable state than distrust. While users with mistrust are likely to develop distrust when they receive additional negative information about a system or when they become victims of actual incidents, users harboring distrust are less likely to move back to a state of mistrust because they have already suffered harm caused by the system.

An individual who trusts an entity has a positive expectation of the entity's future behavior [42, 43]. The individual will cooperate with the entity to reach a certain goal, even though it is possible that the entity will misbehave and inflict costs or damage on the individual. The entity gains the individual's trust over time through repeated actions benefiting the individual.

An individual harboring mistrust believes the uncertainty is too large to expect a particular behavior from an entity. A citizen may, for example, believe in the government's sincere desire to deliver highly secure services on the Web, but has little or no confidence in the government's ability to actually deliver adequate security.

An individual distrusting an entity believes the entity will deliberately act against him or her in a given situation. A citizen harboring distrust may think that the government intentionally overstates the security of its e-government services or uses collected personal information to spy on individuals.

While a citizen's trust in a system can be in one of only three states in this chapter, the whole population has different degrees of trust, mistrust, and distrust at the same time, measured by the fractions of individuals in each of the three states. Note that the three fractions sum to one.

To illustrate a population's mistrust and distrust of an ICT system, as well as its owner, we consider a large identity management system that was never fully implemented. A former UK government under Labour started to deploy a centralized identity system, called the National Identity Scheme (NIS), to provide biometric identity cards to all lawful residents aged 16 and over. Roughly £250 million were spent developing NIS (http://news.bbc.co.uk/2/hi/8707355.stm).

The London School of Economics and Political Science started the Identity Project to analyze NIS. Project members mistrusted the UK government, accusing it of not understanding the political, social, and technological risks of establishing a national ID system with a centralized database containing up to 50 data points per individual [44].

Over the years, the Identity Project published reports and participated in the national debate to convince politicians to scrap NIS. The lobby group NO2ID also opposed the creation of NIS. Their briefing papers imply distrust of the UK government. In particular, NO2ID discussed how NIS could allow the government to manage society by spying on people, severely compromising their privacy and security.

The UK Labour government allowed mistrust and distrust to grow by relegating, ignoring, or attacking independent experts pointing out weaknesses in NIS [44, pp. 81–2], [45]. The predominantly negative press coverage of NIS helped spread mistrust and distrust when people started to discuss it. According to a study of UK newspapers [45], NIS was portrayed as unsafe, lacking accountability, compulsory rather than based on choice, universal, tough on immigration, and creating an imbalance between liberty and security. In 2010, the new Conservative coalition government's Identity Documents Act abolished the identity cards and ordered the destruction of all data in the associated National Identity Register.

## 3.2  Explanatory Trust Model

The following discrete-time model provides an explanation for how trust, mistrust, and distrust change in a population due to incidents in a complex ICT system. Patches on a square represent the modeled individuals. The square wraps around at the edges, that is, the model has a doughnut shape. An individual's state of trust is represented by the color of the patch: Trust is green (■), mistrust is yellow ( ), and distrust is red (■), as seen in Fig. 3.1. Each individual has eight neighbors. At each time step, the state of an individual is updated based on the states of its neighbors.

Since it is not obvious how to update the patches, we study 14 sets of update rules defined by the columns of Table 3.1. Each set has two rules defining changes from trust to mistrust and from mistrust to distrust, as well as two rules defining changes in the opposite directions. The two first (last) rules induce a color change when the number of green neighbors is no larger (no smaller) than a threshold. To clarify, the four rules defined by the rightmost column in Table 3.1 are as follows:

 (i) A green patch changes to yellow when a maximum of four neighbors are green.
 (ii) A yellow patch turns red when a maximum of three neighbors are green.
(iii) A red patch turns yellow when a minimum of seven neighbors are green.
(iv) A yellow patch turns green when a minimum of six neighbors are green.

The two first rules in a set repeatedly reduce a population's trust as individuals become increasingly surrounded by individuals with mistrust or distrust. The rules create an escalating feedback loop producing increasingly more mistrusting and distrusting individuals when the initial conditions are right. The two last rules create a dampening feedback loop when the starting conditions are right, but this time to increase the population's trust.

All 14 rule sets defined by the columns in Table 3.1 result in the same change pattern: An individual with trust goes through a period of mistrust before developing distrust and an individual with distrust develops mistrust before trust. Individuals who have trusted an entity for a long time are reluctant to mistrust or distrust it.

**(a)**                         **(b)**                         **(c)**

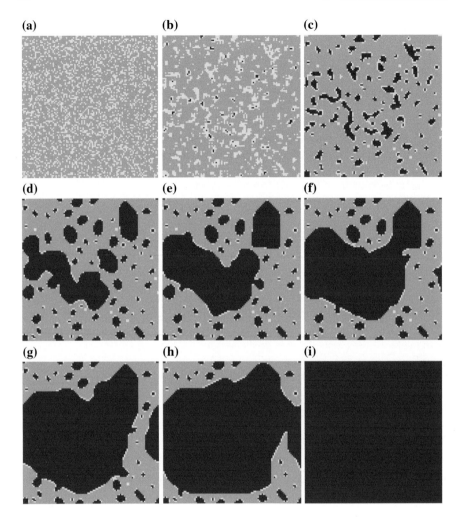

**Fig. 3.1** Development of mistrust in a $100 \times 100$ population of patches. The initial mistrust is 27 % (*yellow patches*) at time step $t = 0$. The following snapshots show the formation and spreading of distrust (*red patches*) over time. Rules (i)–(iv) were used. **a** $t = 0$, **b** $t = 1$, **c** $t = 3$, **d** $t = 20$, **e** $t = 40$, **f** $t = 60$, **g** $t = 80$, **h** $t = 100$, **i** $t = 165$

Distrusting individuals are even more reluctant to ever again trust an entity that has violated their trust and caused pain or damage. Finally, an individual harboring mistrust develops distrust when surrounded by much mistrust.

**Table 3.1** Each column defines a set of four update rules

| Changes | Color-changing thresholds | | | | | | | | | | | | | |
|---|---|---|---|---|---|---|---|---|---|---|---|---|---|---|
| | *Maximum number of green neighbors* | | | | | | | | | | | | | |
| ■ → □ | 3 | 3 | 3 | 3 | 3 | 3 | 3 | 3 | 4 | 4 | 4 | 4 | 4 | 4 |
| □ → ■ | 1 | 1 | 1 | 1 | 2 | 2 | 2 | 2 | 1 | 1 | 2 | 2 | 3 | 3 |
| | *Minimum number of green neighbors* | | | | | | | | | | | | | |
| ■ → □ | 6 | 6 | 7 | 7 | 6 | 6 | 7 | 7 | 6 | 7 | 6 | 7 | 6 | 7 |
| □ → ■ | 5 | 6 | 5 | 6 | 5 | 6 | 5 | 6 | 6 | 6 | 6 | 6 | 6 | 6 |

The two first entries in a column define the maximum number of green neighbors causing changes toward distrust, while the two last entries define the minimum number of green neighbors needed to change away from distrust

## 3.3 Model Limitations

Since a model is a simplification of a real-world system, it is possible to create many models emphasizing different aspects of the real system. We have introduced a simple model of a population's trust in a system. It is possible to add more functionality to this model. As an example, we could equip the individuals with a memory of past incidents. Furthermore, while all individuals react the same way in the current model, it is possible to use different rules for different individuals. Finally, many other update rules are possible.

Alternatively, we could define a trust model by a graph where the nodes represent individuals and the edges connect nodes that influence each other. When the views of experts and commentators are widely reported by the media, a few nodes have a very large number of edges to neighboring nodes. While our model does not include these "super-spreaders"directly, their combined influence is represented by the initial pattern of mistrust. The more negative the media coverage, the higher the percentage of initial mistrust.

The trust model is non-predictive, in the sense that it cannot forecast a population's trust in a real system. However, it offers an explanation of how the degree of trust changes in a large community of users.

## 3.4 Trust Is Fragile

We first study how a high degree of trust can turn into a high degree of distrust. We concentrate on system incidents reported in the media. While most incidents go unnoticed by the media, a few incidents are widely reported. Not all reported events are very serious from a technical point of view, but extensive media coverage can still create mistrust among a significant fraction of users.

The explanatory model was implemented in NetLogo [46] and the highlighted rules (i)–(iv) were used to generate the figures. At the start of a model run, a selectable percentage of all individuals is yellow (mistrust) and the remaining percentage is green (trust). The yellow patches are selected at random. Initially there is no distrust. Figure 3.1 shows snapshots of a model run with an initial mistrust of 27 % in a population of 10,000 patches. Figure 3.1a depicts many small localized outbreaks of mistrust at time step $t = 0$ due to widespread media coverage of an incident. Distrust starts to occur already at time step $t = 1$. The distrust forms isolated islands that start to combine as they become larger. The run ends when the patches' color patterns no longer change. At the end of the run in Fig. 3.1i, there is 100 % distrust.

Figure 3.2 plots the final fraction of distrust as a function of the initial fraction of mistrust. Each column in the plot was averaged over 100 runs with the same initial fraction of mistrust. As long as the initial density of mistrust is less than 15 %, the resulting fraction of distrust is less than 1 %, on average. However, around 15 % of initial mistrust, there is a transition where increasing mistrust rapidly results in very large fraction of distrust. An initial mistrust of 28 % results in 99 % distrust, on average. Experiments with the additional 13 leftmost rule sets in Table 3.1 all revealed similar sharp transitions to massive distrust starting at fairly low percentages (16–33 %) of initial mistrust. Since it is difficult to determine when these transitions occur in real systems, it is hard to predict if an incident will lead to massive distrust.

The model indicates (but does not prove) that user trust in a complex ICT system is fragile, because an incident affecting a few users can create massive distrust when extensive media reporting creates enough initial mistrust. The UK Labour government did not handle the media skillfully. Therefore, extensive negative press helped create enough distrust to stop NIS. Of course, an incident affecting many users directly can create enough initial mistrust without any help from the media. According to the explanatory model, both cases result in pervasive mistrust.

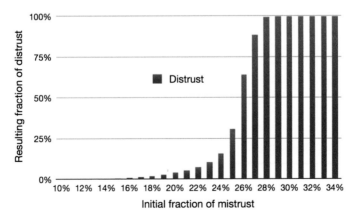

**Fig. 3.2** Average fraction of distrust as a function of the initial fraction of mistrust in a population of $100 \times 100$ patches. A transition starts around 15 %

## 3.5   Distrust Is Robust

Next, we determine when the model moves from a high percentage of distrust to a high percentage of trust. At the start of a model run, all the patches are red, that is, there is 100 % distrust. A selectable percentage of the red patches chosen at random then change to green as the model starts to run. Figure 3.3 plots the resulting percentage of trust as a function of the initial percentage of green patches, again using the rules (i)–(iv) detailed earlier. Each column of the plot is averaged over 100 runs. There is a rapid transition around 80 % initial trust. Below this transition, the model returns to 100 % distrust. The plot demonstrates how hard it is to create widespread trust when there is massive initial distrust.

Experiments with the 13 additional sets of rules in Table 3.1 also showed similar sharp transitions at large values (42–80 %) of initial trust. The model again returns to 100 % distrust below these transitions. The model implies that massive distrust in a complex ICT system is robust to large efforts to create widespread trust. It will take a sustained effort over a long period to rebuild trust. There is no guarantee that such an effort will succeed. In fact, it may be close to impossible to rebuild widespread trust in a system when there is massive distrust among the user population.

A few comments are needed to fully understand both the limitations and implications of all the reported experiments. While it is unlikely that a large population has 100 % trust or distrust in a real system, it is not unlikely that the population's trust varies sharply, as depicted in Figs. 3.2 and 3.3. However, the experiments do not prove that such transitions exist, especially since we have only explored one of many possible trust models and only deployed a tiny fraction of all possible update rules.

Taken together, the reported experiments suggest that a long-term effort to limit the formation of mistrust should already be started when a system is first created. The effort should be intensified immediately after an incident to avoid a state of massive distrust from which it is very hard to recover. A successful effort to build a good

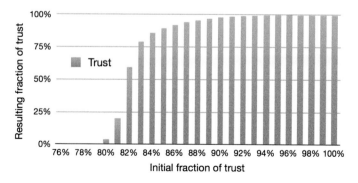

**Fig. 3.3** Average fraction of trust as a function of the initial fraction of trust in a population of $100 \times 100$ patches. A transition starts around 80 %

reputation and to reduce incident reporting translates into a smaller percentage of initial mistrust in the model. As long as the percentage is below the transition point to massive distrust (see Fig. 3.2), the mistrust will die out rather quickly, returning the population to a high level of trust.

## 3.6   Maintaining Trust

Since it is very hard to recover from massive distrust, an anti-fragile organization has to actively build and maintain its customers' trust. This section first discusses the Tylenol crisis in 1982 to illustrate that it is possible to avoid massive loss of trust, even during very challenging situations. It then discusses specific approaches to build and maintain a user population's trust in an ICT system providing digital services, especially an e-government platform delivering services to an entire nation.

The painkiller Tylenol provided about 15 % of Johnson & Johnson's corporate profit during the first three quarters of 1982. Then somebody laced Tylenol capsules with cyanide and killed seven people in the Chicago area. The company quickly stopped Tylenol production and issued warnings to hospitals and distributors. It then recalled about 30 million Tylenol bottles from the market and advertised in the media to warn people not to use the product. Johnson & Johnson put public safety first, even though the recall was very expensive. The company got much positive press for their resolute handling of the crisis. While Johnson & Johnson's share of the painkiller market fell from around 35–8 % after the killings, the company reintroduced the product and rebounded in less than a year.

### 3.6.1   Prepare Alternative Services

Whether or not an ICT system is implemented in the cloud, there is always a possibility of a rare, catastrophic incident taking down the system and all its services for a long time. If there are no alternatives to the services offered by an organization, then a long simultaneous failure of all services is intolerable to the organization, because mistrust (followed by distrust) will spread among users, resulting in demands for technical changes and even financial compensation. Consequently, it is a good idea to have alternative solutions to the most important services to reduce the possibility of mistrust and distrust spreading in the user population. A government could for example run its services in a cloud and use another cloud in an emergency. Alternative services should run continuously. If services lie dormant much of the time, there is a significant chance they will not work when needed. For example, it is not uncommon for emergency power systems to not work because they have not been tested for a long time.

According to Geer [31], it is important to retain pre-Internet systems because they have few external dependencies and avoid common mode failures with Internet-based systems. The dismantling of old systems and procedures that have worked well for decades may have serious unintended consequences. National institutions that no longer accept communication on paper exclude a small but significant percentage of the population. Furthermore, states relying solely on electronic voting cannot fall back on traditional paper voting should the electronic voting solutions fail due to technical problems or targeted attacks. Finally, citizens and first responders in countries dismantling their fixed-line phone systems cannot communicate when the mobile phone systems are down. Much of the costs companies and governments save by eliminating redundant systems may be lost when swan incidents take down their remaining unique systems. While it makes sense to eliminate a redundant system in the short run, it can turn out to be a very bad decision in the long run.

### 3.6.2  Make Digital Services Voluntary

It may be tempting for an organization, especially a government, to "force" individuals to use its digital services. A government can even create a legal obligation to use e-government services to ensure large resource savings. However, the mandatory use of digital services is likely to create mistrust or even distrust because users have little or no control over an organization's actions. Furthermore, some individuals lack the computer skills needed to use the services and others have disabilities forcing them to depend on the help from others. Consequently, it should be possible to opt out of any service without undue difficulty to avoid mistrust and distrust among individuals. In summary, an obligation to use a system leads to mistrust or even distrust, while voluntary use ensures that nearly all new users will trust the system because without trust they will not use it. Since a high fraction of initial trust makes it easier to maintain the necessary trust over time, voluntary use is better than mandatory use.

### 3.6.3  Build a Good Track Record

It is counterproductive for an organization to ignore or hide the fact that events with a negative impact are inevitable in ICT systems of high complexity. It is a particularly bad policy to rely on spin control after incidents have occurred. An organization should, instead, gain trust by creating a good track record from the start of a new service. The dissemination of practical information to users via the Web and the press is a way to build trust.

An organization must demonstrate competence and quickly fix problems when a large incident occurs. If the organization has a good track record, then users are quite forgiving when they are convinced that an incident was caused by a technical problem [42]. Since the loss of trust can be huge when users suspect malicious intent, an organization must clarify its intentions, especially how it will use and not use personal information, to prevent the rapid deterioration of trust during an incident.

## 3.7   Discussion and Summary

To build and maintain an anti-fragile ICT system, it is not enough to use the right system design and the best information technologies; it is also necessary to create an organization that learns from mistakes, values openness, and understands the importance of building and maintaining trust relationships with its customers. If the overall level of trust is high and a system failure is due to an understandable human error or a technical glitch, then customers forgive readily, assuming the organization is open about the cause of the failure and shows competence when rectifying the mistake. An organization that downplays incidents, stonewalls journalists, attacks independent commentators and security experts, and displays arrogance toward its customers risks creating massive distrust in the user population. This chapter illustrates that the organization may be unable to recover from such a position, even if it spends large amounts of resources trying to rebuild trust.

# Chapter 4
# Principles Ensuring Anti-fragility

While it is impossible to predict all potential swan events that can severely impact complex information and communications technology (ICT) systems, we know the general reasons for extreme global behavior: single points of failure such as shared resources, local failures initiating systemic failures due to chain reactions, scaling effects, and cascading failures between system layers and different systems [35, Chap. 4]. Because the removal of single points of failure is a well-understood problem [47], this chapter first introduces four design principles that together isolate local failures before they propagate and cause systemic failures. It then presents one operational principle to quickly remove exploitable vulnerabilities. Finally, the chapter discusses how a systemic failure can occur in a complex adaptive system even when no parts fail, as well as the need to build models to understand such extreme global behavior.

The current chapter defines and illustrates five principles needed to design and operate anti-fragile ICT systems, while the following chapters discuss how these principles can be implemented in different types of complex ICT systems. The principles are rooted in the analysis in Chap. 2, showing the need to isolate local failures and use natural and induced failures to learn about vulnerabilities. The reader may recognize some of the principles as software patterns described in books on software design [35, 48]. Here, we use the term *principle* rather than *pattern* to emphasize that these ideas or concepts can be found in many research fields, not only software design [3, 4, 19, 35, 48, 49, 50].

## 4.1 Modularity

A complex adaptive ICT system with tightly interconnected units tends to exhibit surprising and undesirable global behavior due to the many non-linear interactions between the units [5, 6]. A local failure due to an internal error in a unit or abnormal

© The Author(s) 2016

K.J. Hole, *Anti-fragile ICT Systems*, Simula SpringerBriefs on Computing 1,
DOI 10.1007/978-3-319-30070-2_4

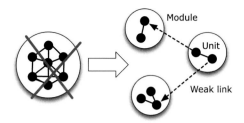

interactions between several units could cause problems for other units and eventually take down the whole system. The first step to avoid propagating local failures in networked computer systems is to modularize the systems at both the hardware and software levels [1, 3, 4]. Conceptually, we represent the modules of a system by nodes in a hierarchical system graph (Figure 4.1 illustrates one level of the graph), where each module is a subgraph of tightly cohesive units.

We use the expressions *strong connection* and *weak connection* to describe the varying levels of dependence between system modules. The terms *dependency* and *connection* are used in much the same way in this book. A module $A$ is *strongly connected* with (or strongly dependent on) a module $B$ if $A$'s functionality is badly affected when $B$ misbehaves or fails. The module $A$ is *weakly connected* (or weakly dependent) if $A$'s important functionality is preserved when $B$ malfunctions or terminates. When modules are weakly connected, a change to a module should not necessitate changes to any other module. The modules must have well-defined interfaces and these interfaces must be the only way modules can interact with each other. In particular, the internal state of a module must not be directly accessible to another module, but only made available via an interaction mechanism that communicates state information. A communication protocol is an important example of an interaction mechanism.

The system graphs in Fig. 4.1 illustrate the transition from a system of tightly interconnected units to a system of weakly connected modules. The units constituting a module depend on the system level being studied. If we study a complete software solution consisting of a set of well-defined software services, then a module is a service and a unit is a collection of subroutines. In a distributed hardware system, for example, a collection of network routers, a printed circuit board is a unit, while a module is a collection of boards that constitute a cohesive part of a hardware device. If we study interconnected systems, then a module is a whole system.

It is important to understand the difference between strong and weak dependencies in modular systems. Strong dependencies were actually first defined in Sect. 2.7, although the definition did not explicitly introduce the concept of strength. The same section stated that the impact of recurrent incidents in a modular system can be mitigated by introducing additional strong dependencies between the modules. Unfortunately, we may introduce new positive feedback loops at the same time, thus increasing the probability of extreme global behavior in the form of nonrecurrent swan incidents. The next section outlines how to avoid swans by limiting the strength of dependencies in modular systems.

## 4.2  Weak Links

When the functionality of a module $\mathcal{A}$ at some system level depends on the functionality of another module $\mathcal{B}$, there is a directed link from $\mathcal{A}$ to $\mathcal{B}$ in the system graph to represent this dependency. In Fig. 4.1, each directed link signifies the relation *depends on*. Different dependencies have varying strengths [5]. We can measure the strength of a dependency by determining the damage a misbehaving module causes in the dependent module.

The next step to prevent local failures from propagating is to ensure that the incoming links to a misbehaving module break in such a way that there is little or no damage to the dependent modules. These so-called *weak links* [49] enhance robustness to propagating failures by restricting damage to a single module. The weak links are represented by dashed lines in Fig. 4.1.

A weak link can be compared to a circuit breaker that protects an electrical system against excessive current. The circuit breaker is an automatic electrical switch designed to detect a fault condition and interrupt current flow. Unlike a fuse, which operates once and then must be replaced, a circuit breaker can be reset to resume normal operation. We are interested in weak links that can restore themselves after they break. Chapter 5 studies how to implement weak links with default fallback responses.

It is necessary to determine the dependencies between modules at different levels of a system [2]. Modules are weakly connected when they have weak links. If the hierarchical system graph of weakly connected modules (see Fig. 4.1) is sparse and of limited size, then the remaining fragility can be analyzed. A dense and large graph of strong dependencies signals intolerable fragility because it becomes hard to determine the cause(s) of an incident and, therefore, countermeasures to avoid similar incidents in the future [4].

## 4.3  Redundancy

According to Taleb [10], redundancy is an inherent property of anti-fragile systems. They do not make "efficiency" their primary goal. Since the goal of anti-fragile systems is to thrive in randomness, the systems contain "inefficiencies" through layered redundancies. Computer systems enhance their robustness to module failures by

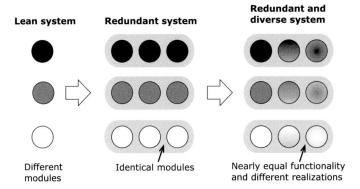

**Fig. 4.2** Transition from a lean system to a redundant system and then to a system with both redundancy and diversity

deploying multiple copies of modules at the software and hardware levels. Figure 4.2 illustrates the transition from a lean system to a redundant system. The redundancy is obtained by introducing extra copies of each module.

Two examples illustrate the redundancy principle. First, when a virtual machine fails in a cloud-based system, an identical instance is started automatically. Second, a critically important system should have at least one secondary backup system that runs in parallel with the primary system to ensure a safe fallback. Leading up to the next principle, we note that the secondary system should differ from the primary system to avoid both failing for the same reasons.

## 4.4  Diversity

A modular system has diversity [50] when it contains differently designed or implemented modules with (nearly) the same functionality. Figure 4.2 depicts the transition from a redundant system to a system that is both redundant and diverse. Diversity makes it less likely that many modules will fail at the same time. Only a diverse system is highly robust to propagating failures; single modules remain fragile. Failures of fragile modules are warning signals of impending systemic instability. If a computer system is a "monoculture," where all computing devices are based on the same hardware or run the same software [28, 29], then it is highly fragile, because a local failure can propagate very easily. This is particularly true for infectious malware that can easily spread to many modules in a large software monoculture. The use of software diversity to halt malware spreading is discussed in Part III.

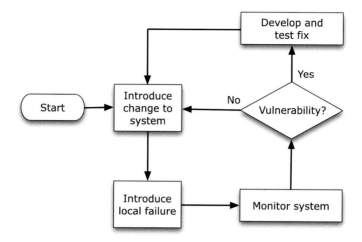

**Fig. 4.3**  How to use the fail fast principle in an ICT system

## 4.5  Fail Fast

To create complex adaptive systems that are anti-fragile to classes of negative events, it is necessary to learn from problems and downright failures in the systems because it is effectively impossible to predict all future incidents with a large negative impact. Hence, a system should fail early when the impact is small and stakeholders should learn from these incidents how to adapt the system to limit the impact of future incidents.

When the four design principles of modularity, weak links, redundancy, and diversity are used to avoid failure propagation, we can induce local failures (with only a tiny probability of systemic failure) to detect vulnerabilities early and quickly learn how to improve the ability to prevent propagating failures. The flow diagram in Fig. 4.3 illustrates how the fail fast principle can be used in a system. Netflix pioneered the depicted technique in its cloud-based subscription service for films and TV series (http://techblog.netflix.com). Chapter 5 will discuss Netflix's realizations of the operational fail fast principle and the four outlined design principles.

## 4.6  Systemic Failure Without Failed Modules

A local failure can propagate over a system and cause a systemic failure. Although there is a strong tendency to assume that a local failure is a well-defined event occurring inside a single module, this is not necessarily true for complex adaptive systems. A well-functioning technical system with normally behaving stakeholders could drift into a systemic failure in the form of a swan event without any well-defined initial

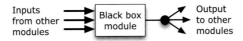

**Fig. 4.4**  A module in a complex adaptive system viewed as a black box with multiple inputs from other modules and a single output connected to yet other modules

module failure. Swans are often caused by internal and external changes that affect the global pattern of interactions between the modules, between the stakeholders, and between the stakeholders and modules. The changes all seem reasonable when studied in isolation. It is only the combination of the changes that causes a systemic failure [18].

To better understand how a systemic failure can occur without any module failure, we consider a module as a black box with multiple input links and a single output link (see Fig. 4.4). A module receives inputs from other modules and generates an output that becomes input to yet other modules. A module is designed to generate particular output values from combinations of specified input values. If a module receives an unknown or a partial combination of inputs that it was not designed to handle, it can produce an extreme output value. When the extreme output becomes input to another module, it can result in another extreme output. Hence, an unusual combination of inputs to a module can cause more and more modules to generate extreme outputs, leading to a systemic failure. This rare and extreme global behavior occurs despite all modules correctly executing their designed input–output transformations, that is, there are no module failures per se.

The reader should note that incomplete or extreme input combinations to modules could occur due to random noise or temporary faults in the communication links. These transient failures can be hard to recreate and may even be completely overlooked during an investigation to determine why a system misbehaved. This is particularly true when multiple transient errors combine to create incomplete or extreme input combinations.

Since classical risk analysis is based on the notion that a large failure is caused by a chain of smaller events initiated by a well-defined starting event, the analysis may not predict the above systemic failure. The classical approach to risk analysis based on simple, or linear, cause and effect thinking only works satisfactorily when the system's parts are weakly connected with limited interaction. Complex adaptive systems are often strongly connected with a great deal of interaction. To understand the risks associated with complex systems, analysts must avoid thinking that restricts failures to simple chains of events, because this approach ignores potential swans and thus seriously underestimates the total risk taken by stakeholders [18].

The earlier stated principle of weak links is critical to avoid failure propagation that is not initiated by a local failure in a single module but caused by an unusual combination of inputs to one or more modules leading to extreme global behavior. Consider a system monitoring its modules to break the output links, perhaps after some delay, when the modules produce extreme output. The modules exist in a (logical) hierarchy, where each module belongs to a particular level. A given module may receive inputs from several modules at a lower level. Even if each of the lower-level modules generates normal output, the combination of values taken as input to the upper-level module may still cause this module to generate extreme output. However, since the module is monitored and stopped when it generates extreme output, a systemic failure is, most likely, avoided.

## 4.7  The Need for Models

While it is quite easy to understand the descriptions of the five principles, it is hard to determine how to realize them in complex adaptive ICT systems to achieve anti-fragility to a particular type of impact. Paraphrasing Yaneer Bar-Yam [51], we argue that it is necessary to create system models, especially during the design phase, to ensure anti-fragility.

The beginning of Chap. 1 discussed the complexity of an ICT system consisting of a large networked computer system and many stakeholders (see Fig. 1.1). The complexity is due to the numerous interactions between the stakeholders and the computer system, the large amounts of communications between the networked subsystems, and the influence of changing security and privacy policies, as well as threats such as equipment failure, extreme weather, and sabotage. An alternative to this communication view of complexity is the behavioral complexity obtained by viewing a complete ICT system as a black box and then studying the minimum amount of information, measured in bits, needed to describe all possible input-output relations.

Let us consider an ICT system with $N_{in}$ input values and $N_{out}$ output values. The values can be in the form of vector or scalar values. We need a minimum of $A = \log_2 N_{out}$ bits to represent an output because all the $2^A$ outputs must have unique descriptions. Similarly, we need $I = \log_2 N_{in}$ bits to uniquely label an input. The labels allow us to order the inputs. Assume that we have an ordered list of $2^I$ entries, where the first entry contains the output corresponding to the first input, the second entry contains the output corresponding to the second input, and so on. Since we need $A$ bits to specify an output, the total number of bits needed to completely describe all input–output relations is $2^I \cdot A$. This expression measures the behavioral complexity of an ICT system.

The idea of classical software development is to build a system that realizes a set of well-defined input–output relations. Before the system goes into production, it must be tested. A complex adaptive ICT system with huge numbers of computational devices and users has a huge number of possible inputs. If, for example, $I = 200$ bits, then the complexity is greater than $2^{200} \approx 10^{60}$ bits, which is an enormous number.

Since it is clearly impossible to exhaustively test all inputs, theory is essential to understand how to realize the five principles in complex adaptive systems. Models are especially useful because they characterize global emergent behaviors without having to test all possible inputs. For systems without adequate models, the limitations of testing lead to significant uncertainty about the systems' global behaviors, especially their fragility to swans. While models help reduce the risk to stakeholders, complex adaptive systems will always have hidden risks due to their highly non-linear and time-varying relations between the inputs and outputs [7]. Hence, as first stated in Sect. 2.5, there is no absolute guarantee that complex ICT systems are swan free.

In Chap. 3, we built a model to understand how a user population's trust in an ICT system could change from pervasive trust to massive distrust. Because of the great behavioral complexity, no effort was made to accurately model all aspects of the trust relationship between users and system operators. Instead, we developed an explanatory toy model. Although toy models cannot predict the detailed behavior of systems, the models can be used to uncover fragility to particular types of impacts.

## 4.8  Discussion

The four design principles of *modularity*, *weak links*, *redundancy*, and *diversity* and the *fail fast* operational principle are not new, since various descriptions can be found in different research fields [3, 4, 19, 35, 48, 49, 50]. However, Taleb's [8, 9, 10] conceptual foundation and the way the principles are melded in Part II outline a novel strategy to design and operate anti-fragile ICT systems.

The reader may wonder if the five principles are sufficient to ensure anti-fragility to any given class of impacts. At the time of this writing, in late 2015, the answer to this question is not fully known. Most likely, the set of principles needed to design and operate an anti-fragile system depends on the type of system and the class of impacts considered. In Parts II and III, we argue that the five principles provide anti-fragility to downtime and malware spreading. More work is required to determine the need for additional principles. A short discussion of possible additional design principles can be found in Chap. 13.

Chapter 3 argued that it is important to build trust between the owner and the users of a system to avoid the formation of massive distrust in the user population after an incident. It is of course possible to introduce an additional operational principle highlighting the importance of building and maintaining trust. Since the rest of the book concentrates on other aspects of anti-fragile systems, it does not contain an explicit trust principle. However, the building of trust should permeate through all work done to create and operate anti-fragile systems, because the loss of trust is an inherent and general threat to all ICT systems that can cause user populations to abandon systems altogether.

**What to learn from Part I**

Part I modeled large ICT systems as complex adaptive systems and explained that positive feedback loops cause extreme global behavior with an intolerable impact. A complex system is fragile, robust, or anti-fragile to a particular class of negative impacts. It is not enough to create a complex system that is robust to a type of impact when the system is new. Because a complex system and its environment change over time, a robust system becomes fragile. While risk management methods can detect and mitigate many negative events, a complex system has too many interactions between its units and modules for a risk analyst to predict all incidents. It is particularly difficult for a group of stakeholders to predict rare and large-impact incidents called gray swans. Even worse, black swans may exist that are totally unpredictable to all stakeholders in the group.

It is necessary to build complex ICT systems that fail early when the impacts are still small and to learn from the remaining small events how to maintain and improve the systems. Four design principles, namely, *modularity*, *weak links*, *redundancy*, and *diversity*, and one operational principle, *fail fast*, were introduced to provide anti-fragility to different types of impact. The common goal of the design principles is to prevent inevitable local failures from propagating into global failures. The goal of the operational principle is to quickly determine vulnerabilities and remove them before they can cause serious damage. Here, a vulnerability can be a flaw in the design, a bug in the implementation, or a mistake in the operation or management of a system.

Because there is no absolute guarantee that a systemic failure will never occur, an owner or operator of a complex ICT system must build and maintain a trust relationship with the customers, especially since it can be argued that trust is fragile and distrust is robust. If a company allows distrust to grow, for example, by relegating, ignoring, or attacking individuals pointing out system weaknesses, then the company may not survive a failure, especially when it is heavily reported in the press.

# Part II
# Anti-fragility to Downtime

# Chapter 5
# Anti-fragile Cloud Solutions

To better understand how to achieve anti-fragility to downtime, the chapters of Part II discuss how to realize the four design principles and the one operational principle from Chap. 4 in different types of systems. The current chapter focuses on how to realize the principles in customer-facing web-scale solutions in the cloud. Much of the discussion is based on design and operational patterns described by Nygard [35] and Netflix's realization of these patterns in its cloud-based streaming service. YouTube videos (http://youtube.com/watch?v=jCanhyFDopQ, https://youtube.com/watch?v=dekV3Oq7pH8) document that the development teams at Netflix used the principles described in Chap. 4 to build and operate an anti-fragile system.

## 5.1 Choice of System Realization

We initially consider the advantage of realizing a web-scale solution in a public cloud compared to a traditional private datacenter. For simplicity, we consider a generic cloud infrastructure offering services to manage virtual machines, data storage, networking, and monitoring. The generic cloud platform is divided into regions, each with multiple availability zones. The zones correspond to different datacenters. All virtual machines run on commodity hardware. Failures happen routinely due to the infrastructure's huge number of servers, storage units, and network equipment [13, 14]. While a company or a government can build a private cloud infrastructure, it is less expensive to use a public cloud, because its cost is divided among many customers. The pay-as-you-go pricing model makes a public cloud especially attractive to startup companies that want to compete with established companies having their own infrastructures.

The architecture of a system models the major components and the important relations between them [52]. Figure 5.1a sketches the architecture of a web-scale solution running in a private datacenter without cloud technologies. This server-side application is said to be *monolithic* because it is built as one entity with a single

© The Author(s) 2016
K.J. Hole, *Anti-fragile ICT Systems*, Simula SpringerBriefs on Computing 1,
DOI 10.1007/978-3-319-30070-2_5

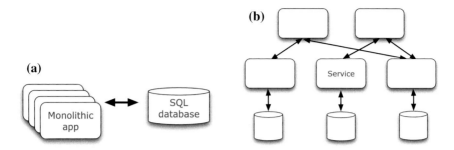

**Fig. 5.1  a** Replicated monolithic application running on multiple servers in a private datacenter. All application copies use the same database. **b** Identical application functionality realized by self-contained services running on a cloud platform and storing data in databases replicated over multiple zones

executable [53, 54]. One or more load balancers (not shown) distribute requests to replicated executables that run on multiple servers. All application copies use the same database. Figure 5.1b sketches a service-oriented architecture (SOA) with layers of self-contained services running on a cloud platform. Together, the services provide the same functionality as the monolithic application. The services use individual databases replicated in multiple zones. Each service is scaled individually by running multiple copies.

The *availability* of a web-scale solution is measured by the percentage of time it is accessible to users. A high availability of 99.99 %, referred to as four nines of availability, corresponds to about 53 min of downtime each year. A solution's *scalability* refers to the number of concurrent users who are having a positive experience and its *performance* refers to the experience of individual users, often measured by response time (latency) [14]. A customer-facing web-scale solution must have high availability to avoid customer dissatisfaction, high scalability to support tens of millions of customers, and good performance to quickly respond to the real-time requests of each customer.

Monolithic (non-cloud) solutions with multiple load balancers and many servers have good scalability up to a point, beyond which scalability becomes exceedingly difficult. The strongly connected modules in the software layer and the high integration of subsystems in the hardware layer also ensure low-latency communication. However, tight integration in both layers leads to propagating failures resulting in insufficient availability. As we shall see, SOA in the cloud provides an efficient way to leverage the redundancy and diversity needed to break the strong dependencies in monolithic solutions. Furthermore, server virtualization on a massive hardware platform supports almost unlimited (horizontal) scalability and the use of multiple cloud regions facilitates low-latency service throughout the world.

## 5.2   Modularity via Microservices

To achieve anti-fragility to downtime, it is not enough to move a monolithic solution into a cloud. It is vital to build a cloud-native solution that takes full advantage of the cloud's properties [13, 14]. In particular, the choice of application architecture is vital to achieve a high degree of anti-fragility to downtime. SOA introduces modularity in the form of well-defined and self-contained services in the software layer. In the hardware layer, the cloud supports modularity by having many availability zones and by assigning multiple zones to each region, where the regions cover different parts of the world.

Netflix's streaming application is based on a fine-grained SOA with *microservices* running in the Amazon Web Services (AWS) cloud. Each of the microservices focuses on doing one thing well. They are combined to provide the needed functionality. In early 2014, the Netflix solution had roughly 600 microservices running side by side in each cloud region. The services are responsible for handling customer-facing requests via a few edge services. The large geographical spread of AWS's regions enables Netflix to offer low-latency, high-throughput media streaming in many countries.

While there is no generally agreed upon definition of microservices, it is possible to describe common properties [53, 54]. A microservice encapsulates a well-defined functionality of value in a business context. The functionality fulfills a single purpose. A microservice runs as a separate process with fast startup and shutdown times. Services can be tested, upgraded, and replaced independently of each other. Finally, a microservice manages its own data. Together, microservices separate the functionality of a large application into highly independent chunks of code. They communicate via a standardized set of simple protocols. The services can be written in different languages and utilize different storage technologies. As we shall see, microservices enhance fault tolerance, enable an application to scale, and allow a solution to evolve.

## 5.3   Weak Links via Circuit Breakers

Virtual machines running (micro-) services are modules in the cloud's software layer. To stop and start the virtual machines without significantly degrading the user experience, they need to be autonomous and stateless. Application state must be stored externally to the machines. If the application state is distributed over many storage devices, then it is possible to upgrade these hardware devices without halting the application.

Weak links are implemented using the *circuit breaker* pattern to ensure that the services are weakly connected [35]. No service contacts another service directly; instead, a service is called via a circuit breaker. The circuit breaker quickly detects when a service develops a problem and open s the circuit (breaks the weak link) to stop the problem from propagating to other services and to provide calling services with a default fallback response. The circuit closes after the problem is fixed. Because

**Fig. 5.2** State diagram for a
generic circuit breaker

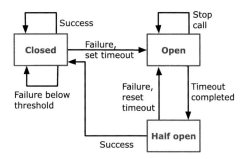

the circuit breaker fails fast, it controls the failure mode, facilitating the graceful
degradation of a system's functionality to limit the damage to users. Note that the
circuit breaker prevents any positive feedback loop from escalating a local failure
into a systemic failure.

Figure 5.2 shows a state diagram of a generic circuit breaker. In the normal closed
state, the circuit breaker is closed and a calling service is allowed to connect to the
called service. If there is a failure, the circuit breaker records it. Once the number,
or frequency, of failures reaches a certain threshold, the circuit trips and opens the
circuit. When the circuit is open, all calls are stopped. After a certain time in the
open state, the circuit breaker moves to the half-open state, which allows the next
calling service to connect to the called service. If this trial call succeeds, then the
circuit breaker returns to the normal closed state. However, should the trial fail,
the circuit breaker returns to the open state until another timeout elapses. To learn
more about circuit breakers, the interested reader should study Netflix's open source
implementation of the pattern (http://github.com/Netflix/Hystrix/wiki).

## 5.4   Redundancy Provided by the Cloud

The cloud supports redundancy at the virtual machine, zone, and region layers. At the
virtual machine layer, a web-scale solution runs redundant machines with timeout
and failover, as illustrated in Fig. 5.3. Multiple virtual machines run the same (micro-)
service in a single availability zone. Figure 5.3a depicts a service depending on one
of the redundant services. When the contacted redundant service times out, another
is queried. The arrows show the direction of the dependencies. Failure of an instance
is often due to power outage in the hosting rack, a disk failure, or a network partition
that cuts off access. When there is a software bug or network failure, all instances
are affected and a (non-personalized) default response is necessary to contain the
error. Careful analysis is needed to determine the appropriate response. Figure 5.3b
illustrates the timeout with a default fallback response.

At the zone layer, failure in one zone should not affect the operation of other
zones. Multiple zones in a single region provide redundancy, as shown in Fig. 5.4. The

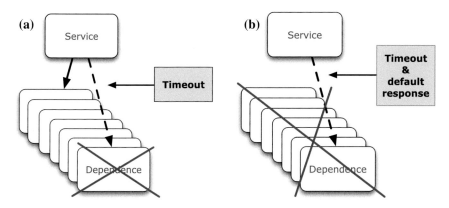

**Fig. 5.3  a** When a service instance times out, another instance is queried. **b** If all instances fail, then there is a default response. The *arrows* show the direction of dependency

**Fig. 5.4**  Use of multiple zones to isolate a zone failure

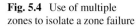

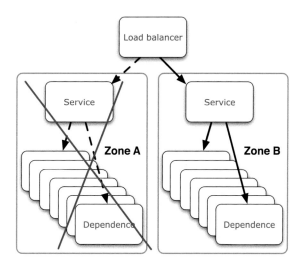

redundancy isolates the consequences of firmware failures, certain serious software bugs, power failures, and severe network failures that take down a whole zone. A web-scale solution should use multiple zones in each region. To compensate for a failed zone, the solution could scale up the remaining zones or introduce a new zone. Note that the load balancer is a single point of failure in Fig. 5.4.

A whole region could fail due to configuration issues, bugs in the infrastructure code, bugs in the application code, and failures in the load balancer. A failed region should not affect other regions. Figure 5.5 depicts two regions, where a server for the domain name system (DNS) splits the traffic load in two halves. A solution should switch users to a new region when needed.

While the redundancy of executable code is important, the data replication obtained by storing the same data on multiple storage devices is critical to achieve

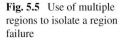

**Fig. 5.5** Use of multiple regions to isolate a region failure

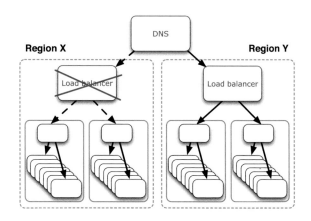

high availability. A cloud infrastructure with a highly redundant network and data storage provides both high availability and extremely high durability, that is, only a tiny probability of data loss. Netflix goes to great lengths to ensure the availability and durability of its data. First, Netflix uses an Apache Cassandra database (http://cassandra.apache.org) that stores data in three zones per region. Cassandra provides NoSQL persistent data storage with eventual consistency [55]. It also supports asynchronous cross-region replication.

Furthermore, Netflix stores backups in the Amazon Simple Storage Service (S3), which is designed to provide 99.99 % availability and 99.999999999 % durability of data objects over a given year, though there is no service-level agreement for durability. The S3 service redundantly stores data in multiple facilities and on multiple devices within each facility. An application is first informed about successful storage after the data are stored across all facilities (http://aws.amazon.com/s3/details). Finally, Netflix copies data in S3 to a storage service run by another cloud provider.

## 5.5   Diversity Enabled by the Cloud

Two software programs are diverse if they have (nearly) the same functionality but different designs or implementations, that is, different machine code [24, 56]. We utilize software diversity to isolate failures by switching between diverse codes, especially when introducing updated services.

Since a web-scale solution supports users throughout the world, there is no good time to take down the whole system to upgrade its software. An alternative is to introduce new code by keeping both old and new code running and switch user requests to the new code. An early version of an updated service is called a *canary*, referring to a canary in a coal mine. The stability of a canary cannot be fully evaluated before it is exposed to a heavy traffic load in a production system. Figure 5.6 illustrates a simple

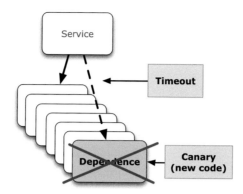

**Fig. 5.6** A simple canary push

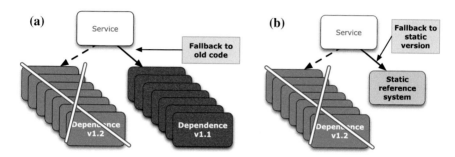

**Fig. 5.7 a** *Red–black* push. **b** Fallback to the static version

canary push where a single instance of an updated service is put into production. If a failure occurs, the system switches back to the old service.

It is possible to extend a simple canary push to include many instances of an updated service. Figure 5.7a illustrates a so-called red–black push where multiple instances of an updated service are needed to carry the traffic load. Instances of the old service are also running to ensure that the system handles peak load if there is a problem with the new code. Note that the cloud facilitates this process because it is easy to double the use of resources for a limited period, for example, a 24-h cycle.

Several versions of a service may contain a "time bomb" that only goes off after a long period. There could be a software bug in both the red and black deployments in Fig. 5.7a or there could be a problem with the data causing several versions of the code to fail. As shown in Fig. 5.7b, it is possible to independently author a static service with simple functionality that delivers a minimal solution when all recent versions of the code fail.

## 5.6  Fail Fast Using Software Tools

To protect and extend companies' market share, web-scale solutions must support rapid scaling and innovation. Since the rate, or frequency, of hardware failures increases as more hardware is added and the rate of software failures increases as the rate of change grows, frequent hardware and software failures are inevitable in web-scale solutions. The engineers at Netflix do not wait for failures to happen. Instead they use a collection of tools, called the *Simian Army*, to deliberately introduce failures into their production system to quickly learn about vulnerabilities and then make changes to ensure that the vulnerabilities do not cause systemic failures (http://techblog.netflix.com/2011/07/netflix-simian-army.html).

The Chaos Monkey tool disables randomly selected virtual machines to make sure the Netflix solution survives this common type of failure without any customer impact. Latency Monkey introduces random latencies between services to simulate network degradation and to ensure that services tolerate latency spikes and other networking issues. The shutdown of a low-level dependency can lead to a longer timeout at a higher layer, causing a cascading failure. Because there is no general answer to this multi-level dependency problem, each case must be carefully studied. Chaos Gorilla generates zone failures and Chaos Kong generates region failures to test that the system survives such rare incidents with a huge impact.

Netflix's preferred approach to failure detection supports Taleb's [9] well-founded claim that it is impossible to predict all rare incidents with a huge negative impact in complex adaptive systems. Instead of trying to predict gray swans, Netflix simply tests its system on a continuous basis to maintain isolation of local failures as the system changes, especially to avoid propagating failures causing downtime. Netflix engineers run the Simian Army tools during the business day to learn about vulnerabilities in the system and to address any immediate problems. If appropriate, the engineers build an automatic recovery mechanism to deal with a newly discovered vulnerability, so that next time a failure occurs no user will notice.

Since silent failures inhibit learning, failures must be detected to prevent a system from becoming increasingly fragile over time. It is necessary to monitor the system's behavior, especially behavioral changes due to system updates. Netflix has built a telemetry system that monitors many different aspects of the system behavior. As an example, a tool using telemetry data determines whether a canary is doing well. There also exist monkeys to monitor the system, such as Security Monkey (http://techblog. netflix.com/2014/06/announcing-security-monkey-aws-security.html) and Conformity Monkey (http://techblog.netflix.com/2013/05/conformity-monkey-keeping-your-cloud.html). This extensive monitoring allows Netflix to constantly adjust its system to keep within the bounds of normal operation.

## 5.7 Top–Down Design and Bottom–Up Tinkering

Before leaving Netflix, we consider the collective impact of the five principles. The four design principles essentially prescribe a *top–down* (reductionist) design approach breaking a new system down into modules and then adding weak links between the modules, thus isolating the impact of local failures. Finally, redundancy and diversity are added to further limit the impact of local failures.

A company $C$ with a system of weakly connected modules that are constantly monitored and tested according to the fail fast operational principle has a competitive advantage over a company $D$ with a system of strongly connected modules. Company $C$ can tinker with its system in a *bottom–up* manner without causing system downtime due to the propagation of local failures. At Netflix, many engineering teams constantly innovate their services without any central coordination of new releases. The teams introduce new features and product enhancements rapidly and frequently. It is hard for company $D$ to maintain a similar high rate of innovation because the many strong dependencies between the modules in their system require the preparation of large coordinated software releases.

Together, the five principles facilitate local decision making in highly independent developer teams. These teams need not schedule common software releases as long as they inform all affected teams about any increased use of computational resources and changes to programming interfaces.

## 5.8 Discussion and Summary

Netflix's web-scale implementation of its media streaming solution with anti-fragility to downtime is evidence that the cloud facilitates the implementation of the design principles of modularity, weak links, redundancy, and diversity and the fail fast operational principle presented in Chap. 4. The generality of the cloud-based realization presented indicates that other large solutions can benefit from Netflix's approach. The next chapters present more systems for which the cloud simplifies the creation of anti-fragility to downtime. Part III shows that the principles also create anti-fragility to malware spreading.

Although the cloud represents a golden opportunity to develop and operate anti-fragile systems, it is not a panacea. A highly competent cloud provider must be selected, preferably with cloud regions throughout the world. Since a major security breach is unacceptable, it is particularly important that the cloud platform limit the consequences of attacks. Finally, any anti-fragile application must be able to handle a situation in which all datacenters in a region go down at the same time.

It is interesting to observe how the design and operational principles together enable safe bottom–up tinkering without the central coordination of different development teams. This advantage can accelerate innovation compared to more traditional software development methods requiring large coordinated software releases.

# Chapter 6
# Toward an Anti-fragile e-Government System

Design is the process of defining a system's components, interfaces, data formats, data flows, and data storage solutions that together satisfy specified availability, performance, and scalability requirements. Chapter 4 introduced four design principles—modularity, weak links, redundancy, and diversity—and a single operational principle, fail fast, to achieve anti-fragility to a class of incidents. Chapter 5 showed how Netflix implemented the five principles to implement a media streaming system with anti-fragility to downtime. To investigate the generality of the five principles, the following two chapters investigate the design of systems to determine how they can be redesigned to achieve a degree of anti-fragility to downtime.

Here, we first study the Norwegian electronic government (e-government) system Altinn as it appeared in 2012 to better understand why it is advantageous to base the design of anti-fragile web-scale systems on fine-grained service-oriented architectures (SOAs) in public clouds with scalable and distributed data storage. This study is partly based on two analyses of Altinn commissioned by the Norwegian Ministry of Trade and Industry [57, 58]. Next, we consider the United Kingdom's e-government system to understand the need for user-focused and iterative development to support both rapid change and high availability. Finally, we discuss whether a nation should have a single e-government system running many services or multiple independent and diverse systems running a few services each.

## 6.1 The Norwegian e-Government System

The Norwegian government has made a large and sustained effort to develop world-leading e-government services for both citizens and companies [59]. Applications, invoicing, appointments, and various types of reports are all handled electronically. These digital services run on the Altinn platform. Sensitive personal information such as tax data are sent over the Internet to personal computing devices, including smartphones and tablets.

© The Author(s) 2016
K.J. Hole, *Anti-fragile ICT Systems*, Simula SpringerBriefs on Computing 1,
DOI 10.1007/978-3-319-30070-2_6

Leading Norwegian politicians believe that most citizens prefer the new digital services to the old paper-based services [60]. The Web will be the primary communication channel between the Norwegian population and the public sector. While it will still be possible for private citizens to call or visit public sector offices, the government wants to minimize traditional person-to-person communications to free up resources needed to bring more and better health care services to Norway's aging population [59, 60]. Hence, high availability is increasingly important to Altinn as more services are added to the platform.

The 2012 version of the platform, denoted Altinn II, is depicted in Fig. 6.1a [57, 58]. A load balancer assigns requests to random servers that run user services. Note that the load balancer is a single point of failure. As illustrated in Fig. 6.1b, each user service is built on top of standardized components provided by the Altinn II platform. Multiple user services utilize the same component. Each component is assigned to a database. Altinn II allows government entities to develop and test their own user services. Scaling takes place by adding more servers and databases.

Despite the Altinn organization's best efforts, the platform's availability has been disappointingly low. The platform had to be taken offline for several days in 2011 and 2012 due to excessive network traffic when the Norwegian Tax Administration published the yearly tax statements. The damage to user trust was particularly noteworthy in 2012 because of the previous year's downtime and because many taxpayers were shown two individuals' names and national ID (IDentity) numbers when they tried to view their own tax statements. Due to some unknown failure, the names and ID numbers were cached and transmitted by the load balancer in Fig. 6.1a. While it can be argued that an ID number is not sensitive information, the national media reported extensively on this "crisis" and a later survey showed that the Altinn organization lost significant trust among its users. The incidents confirm the need to build and maintain trust, as discussed in Chap. 3.

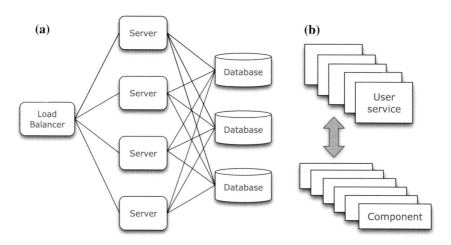

**Fig. 6.1  a** Altinn II architecture. **b** Layers of components and user services

## 6.2  Redesign Needed

The following analysis explains why the Altinn II platform must be redesigned to achieve anti-fragility to downtime. First, since each component in Fig. 6.1b is assigned a particular database, the speed at which a component can read or write data is limited by the capacity of a single database. As the amount of users and services increases, more processes will compete for access to each database because of the fixed component–database assignments [57, 58]. This database bottleneck makes it increasingly hard to scale the system by running more copies of the software on additional hardware. After some years, the system must be redesigned to handle more services and data.

Second, the Altinn II platform periodically runs batch jobs that lock up access to the databases. There is evidence that as the amount of data increases, the batch jobs will take longer to complete, further reducing the system's performance. Finally, Altinn II violates a fundamental tenet of SOA, namely, that user services should be independent of each other. Since dependencies exist between different user services, the failure of one service can negatively affect another. The dependencies also make it hard to upgrade certain user services without taking down the whole system.

In conclusion, while the design of Altinn II is supposedly based on SOA, the real design is database-centric with fragility to downtime due to the database bottleneck and the strong dependencies between software modules. The single load balancer is also problematic. A redesign based on the design principles of modularity, weak links, redundancy, and diversity introduced in Chap. 4 is needed to make the system robust to downtime. The redesign should be carried out by teams experienced in developing, operating, and maintaining web-scale systems, preferably using the development and operations (DevOps) methodology [37, 38]. The teams need to choose highly distributed and scalable data storage solutions to support additional user services with very high availability requirements.

## 6.3  Better Testing

It is much more demanding to test a platform that supports many services of national importance than to test a single enterprise application. The Altinn organization did not have an adequate test environment and test procedures in 2012 [57, 58]. The testing was inadequate in all phases of the development process and the ability to rectify discovered errors was limited. While Altinn was responsible for testing the components, the service owners were responsible for testing the services built on top of the components. The testing tools available to the service owners were not satisfactory. Because of insufficient testing, many bugs were not detected in the code before it went into production. In addition, due to budgetary constraints, many known defects in the production code were not rectified [57].

DevOps teams creating a new solution must improve testing during development. To learn from mistakes and achieve anti-fragility to downtime, the teams must also realize the fail fast operational principle introduced in Chap. 4.

## 6.4  Availability Requirements

A redesigned Altinn platform must satisfy well-defined availability, performance, and scalability requirements [57, 58]. Since this part of the book is concerned with anti-fragility to downtime, we only consider availability requirements. While the following requirements are obvious consequences of the problems with the Altinn II platform, they are valid for many types of platforms, including cloud computing platforms, where stakeholders run their own services:

1. A failure in a (user) service must not affect other services.
2. It must be possible to upgrade a service without system downtime.
3. It must be possible to launch a new service without system downtime.
4. Failure in a component must only affect services that use the component.
5. Good development and testing tools must be available to all developers.

## 6.5  Fine-Grained SOA in a Public Cloud

Achieving high availability is increasingly difficult the more complex a system becomes. Therefore, it is necessary to evolve a highly available web-scale solution, such as an e-government platform with important services, from a smaller, highly available system. Since no complex software system is perfect when first released, updates are needed to satisfy the availability requirements. It is both easier and faster to update the software when it is possible to change selected code modules without having to prepare a major new software release with all the testing it entails. Not all changes to a module lead to desired system behavior. Hence, weakly connected modules, that is, weak links, are essential to limit the negative impact of unintended behavior. Weak links let developers tinker with modules until the desired behavior is achieved. Tinkering makes it easier and faster to make the right changes and to avoid fragility to downtime at the same time.

The above discussion, as well as Netflix's experience discussed in Chap. 5, demonstrate that SOA with well-defined and self-contained services is an appropriate architecture for achieving anti-fragility to downtime. Furthermore, it makes sense to design microservices with limited functionality because it is hard to create default fallback responses for large services, each with much functionality [53, 54].

Since it is very expensive to acquire and maintain the computing hardware needed to support a web-scale solution, virtualization technology should be deployed to achieve reasonable costs [13]. Operating system-level virtualization supports a highly scalable system of many independent computing devices, making it possible to allocate and use idle computing resources more efficiently than in a traditional datacenter without virtualization technology. Rather than building and maintaining a private cloud, a government should seriously consider using a public cloud because its total cost is divided among many entities. We conclude the following:

- To achieve anti-fragility to downtime, governments should base e-government platforms and services on a fine-grained SOA in public clouds with highly redundant and scalable data storage.

## 6.6  User-Focused and Iterative Development

The external Altinn evaluations [57, 58] indicate a need for more user-focused and iterative development to adapt services to users' needs and make the services easier to use [37, 38]. The ability to quickly modify software is also important to mitigate problems and achieve anti-fragility to downtime. In the United Kingdom, there is a unit within the Cabinet Office, called the Government Digital Service (GDS), tasked with transforming government digital services according to users' needs (http://gds. blog.gov.uk). The GDS works with government departments to develop user services, promotes open source development philosophies, and ensures that services are built on open standards and application programming interfaces. The reader can find more information about GDS's development methodology in the Digital by Default Service Standard and its accompanying manual (http://gov.uk/service-manual).

The GDS utilizes the DevOps methodology to break down the traditional silos of development, quality assurance, and operations. The goal is to foster an attitude of shared ownership and collaboration, resulting in common working practices in designing and operating a software solution (http://infoq.com/news/2015/03/gds-uk-gov-devops). GDS has successfully moved the Web presence of all UK government departments to gov.uk [61]. This Web platform publishes government information and provides access to online services. To build e-government services that citizens will use, the GDS has found that developers first need to thoroughly understand the users' needs. Rather than make assumptions, developers must analyze real data from similar services and interview future users to determine their needs. To maintain usability, developers need to revisit services and make alterations as users' needs change over time.

Any service should be designed around the identified users' needs. According to the GDS, developers should start small and iterate often. Frequent iterations reduce the probability of big failures and turn small failures into lessons. It is essential to release prototype solutions early, test them with real users, and move from alpha to beta releases while adding features and refinements based on user feedback.

Viewing e-government infrastructures as complex adaptive systems partly explains the GDS's success with the DevOps methodology. Since it is very hard to predict the long-term global behavior of complex systems, iterative and test-driven approaches are needed to ensure the sufficient availability, scalability, and performance of new services. Experience with Altinn shows that insufficient testing leads to undetected errors, causing trust-reducing incidents [57]. Even worse, shortcomings of the underlying platform architecture go undetected, making it increasingly difficult and costly to satisfy the design requirements as the numbers of users and services grow.

## 6.7  Single Versus Multiple Systems

Should a nation have a single e-government platform running many services or multiple diverse and independent platforms running a few services each? The following answer builds on arguments first presented in an earlier paper [34]. In all the cases discussed, the services access sensitive personal information, including financial and medical data.

### 6.7.1  Systems with Strongly Connected Modules

We first consider e-government systems with strongly connected modules. Each system runs in a traditional datacenter without cloud technologies. We compare a scenario in which a nation employs a single system providing many services with a scenario in which the same nation uses multiple diverse systems providing a few services each. As long as no swan events cause prolonged downtime, the single system exploits economies of scale. Additionally, users enjoy a high degree of usability because the single system lets them authenticate with numerous services using the same authentication technique. Finally, a common user interface design for all services further enhances usability and helps attract many users.

Deploying diverse e-government systems increases the overall burden of system management. The user experience suffers because users must relate to multiple authentication techniques and user interface designs. Consequently, the number of citizens using the online services can decrease. Therefore, a single system is the preferred scenario, barring any black or gray swans.

The situation changes radically when a swan occurs that leads to prolonged downtime. Suddenly, the government is in trouble with millions of citizens, who all want to know what happened and what the government is going to do about the intolerable situation. Because no alternative to the single system exists, it can take a long time before financial and medical information becomes available again. The delay can cause intolerable problems for all users dependent on the information. Therefore, in a swan-prone world, multiple diverse e-government systems are significantly less risky to major stakeholders than a single centralized system, as long as we compare e-government systems with strongly connected modules that run in traditional datacenters.

The choice between building a single or multiple e-government systems with strongly connected modules is essentially the choice between accepting rare, catastrophic events and more frequent, less serious incidents. A nation should, therefore, employ a single strongly connected system only after a thorough and comprehensive risk analysis concludes that all major stakeholders can tolerate swans. If a single system is the solution, the system owner can improve resistance to swans by removing single points of failure and decreasing susceptibility to cascade failures. However, it will be very expensive to obtain the system redundancy and diversity needed to significantly reduce the probability of swans.

While the risk of swans is mitigated by deploying multiple independent and diverse e-government systems running a few services each, it may also be necessary to have two systems delivering the same critically important service. The experience of the Norwegian Food Safety Authority demonstrates the advantage of an alternative solution when a system goes down. The Authority provides a service on the Altinn II platform to allow Norwegian fish exporters obtain export licenses. The Authority produces export licenses for fish worth about 60 billion Norwegian kroner (NOK) in a year. When Altinn went down for several days in 2012, the Authority used an alternative service to produce export licenses, thus protecting the Norwegian fishing industry from large financial losses.

## 6.7.2 Cloud-Based Systems of Weakly Connected Modules

The main advantage of the cloud is that an application owner can achieve the redundancy and diversity of multiple independent implementations in traditional datacenters without actually having to develop and maintain multiple diverse applications. Large public clouds, such as Google App Engine, Amazon Web Services, and Microsoft Azure, are highly geographically distributed infrastructures with regions on different continents, each with multiple zones (datacenters). As demonstrated by Netflix, a cloud-native solution that takes full advantage of a cloud's services can create a single application with very high uptime. Hence, there is much less need to implement multiple independent and diverse versions of an application when it is possible to make a cloud-native application.

While a single cloud platform provides the needed uptime for most services, governmental e-voting services that allow citizens to vote over the Internet during general elections may be an exception to the rule of using only one cloud platform. Since there are indications that citizens are particularly sensitive to failures in voting systems, a government should have an independent voting alternative in case a cloud-based e-voting service has a major outage. In Norway, citizens in certain municipalities have been allowed to vote over the Internet for multiple weeks during elections [7, 43]. The long voting period was selected to reduce the impact of shorter outages because citizens could easily vote later. Furthermore, any citizen could cast a paper vote on the traditional election day, invalidating any earlier cast e-vote. Hence, e-voting did not replace paper-based voting; it only provides an additional means of voting.

To conclude, it is necessary to have multiple and diverse e-government platforms running relatively few services each when each platform solution is strongly connected and run in a traditional datacenter. When a cloud-native solution provides the e-government services, one solution is enough, unless we are talking about very critical e-government services such as e-voting for national elections. In this case, the most critical services need to have independent backup solutions [43, 62]. The reader should keep in mind that no solution can scale forever; scaling will eventually introduce fragility to downtime because the inevitable increase in complexity will introduce unforeseen and fragilizing dependencies [2].

## 6.8  Discussion and Summary

An information and communications technology (ICT) system's mean time to repair (MTTR) is the average time from when a failure occurs until it is repaired and the mean time between failures (MTBF) is the average time between two consecutive failures. While operators of traditional monolithic ICT systems typically try to minimize the MTTR or maximize the MTBF, this is both difficult and costly because the strong dependencies between system modules facilitate local failure propagation leading to expensive systemic failures. There is a need for a better way to build and operate complex adaptive ICT systems with a degree of anti-fragility to downtime.

The increasing popularity of cloud computing and the DevOps methodology facilitate the realization of SOA with microservices that model software applications as sets of independently deployable and scalable services with well-defined interfaces [53, 54]. Circuit breakers remove much of the problem of cascading failures and the use of microservices with limited functionality makes it possible to ensure the graceful degradation of an application's functionality. The limited functionality of each service facilitates the development of automated fallback responses in the case of local failures. When a local failure affects a service, other services depending on this malfunctioning service receive a standardized response. This architectural style also supports the development and management of services by multiple teams using different programming languages; continuous deployment, enabling rapid innovation; and highly redundant and scalable data storage, making data loss extremely unlikely.

While traditional monolithic solutions struggle to achieve high availability, the success of Netflix and other organizations such as Nike and the British newspaper *The Guardian* show that SOA with microservices is well suited to ICT infrastructures requiring high availability. However, it is too early to conclude that this architectural style is the future of huge enterprise and governmental solutions because serious weaknesses may first emerge only after solutions have been in production for years.

For now, we conclude that cloud-based solutions with SOA and microservices can achieve anti-fragility to downtime. At the same time, it seems more difficult and much more expensive to build monolithic applications outside the cloud with anti-fragility to downtime.

# Chapter 7
# Anti-fragile Cloud-Based Telecom Systems

While Netflix has demonstrated how to apply the five design and operational principles to develop and maintain anti-fragile software applications in the cloud, it is less clear whether the cloud facilitates the creation of anti-fragile telecom systems, because nobody has built such a system. Since we need to understand what makes a system fragile to downtime before we can make it anti-fragile, this chapter initially studies the properties of Norwegian telecom infrastructures resulting in fragility to unplanned downtime.

We first introduce three general concepts causing fragility to downtime. Next, we use the concepts to describe examples of Norwegian telecom systems' past fragility to downtime. Then, we create toy models to determine indicators of fragility to future downtime at different levels of the systems. While the models cannot predict extreme global behaviors leading to downtime in the systems, they have enough explanatory power to clarify existing vulnerabilities.

Armed with an understanding of properties that make telecom infrastructures fragile to downtime, we consider how to build and maintain anti-fragile telecom systems with much of the functionality, but not all, implemented in the cloud. We first discuss how the four design principles of modularity, weak links, redundancy, and diversity make telecom infrastructures more robust to downtime, before discussing how the fail fast operational principle makes the infrastructures anti-fragile to downtime.

As the complexity of a system increases, unintended dependencies occur and new levels and patterns emerge, changing the global behavior in unpredictable ways [2]. In particular, new dependencies can create positive feedback loops, making extreme global behavior more likely. Hence, whenever possible, we should remove fragilizing dependencies between modules rather than add new structures and functionality to combat fragility to downtime. The chapter's last part pays special attention to the removal of strong dependencies.

Since a large effort, far beyond the scope of this book, is needed to ensure highly anti-fragile infrastructures to all types of negative impacts, this chapter only points the way toward anti-fragility to downtime. The question of how to use cloud computing in

© The Author(s) 2016
K.J. Hole, *Anti-fragile ICT Systems*, Simula SpringerBriefs on Computing 1,
DOI 10.1007/978-3-319-30070-2_7

telecom systems is an active research area [63, 64]. Because there is no commercially available cloud-based telecom solution, the current chapter is more speculative than Chap. 5 analyzing Netflix's media streaming solution.

## 7.1 Anti-principles Causing Fragility to Downtime

To guide our search for fragility, we exploit so-called *anti-principles* describing how not to design systems. While the existence of black swans make it impossible to precisely quantify a complex system's degree of anti-fragility to a class of impacts, we can easily detect when a system is fragile to a particular class using anti-principles [7, 10, 34]. The following three anti-principles outline how to create fragility to downtime. The author discusses these anti-principles in an earlier paper [7]. The current versions are slightly modified to emphasize downtime in telecom infrastructures.

**Uniqueness**    A system is unique when its key services are not provided by another system. A unique infrastructure with strong dependencies between modules and little redundancy and diversity—the extreme case being a traditional monoculture [28, 29]—is particularly fragile to downtime because local failures spread easily and its many users cannot switch to an alternative infrastructure during an outage.

**Connectedness**    A system is connected when its normal operation depends on the normal operation of another system. If an infrastructure is connected to another infrastructure, then the large overall complexity of the infrastructures causes fragility to downtime.

**Closed**    A system is closed when stakeholders do not share technical and legal information. If only a small group of experts have deep knowledge of an infrastructure, they have a tendency to develop similar mental models for how the infrastructure works during discussions. This propensity toward groupthink is especially strong when most group members belong to the same organizational culture. A uniform group cut off from external expertise with different perspectives overlooks possible rare events causing downtime.

Similar to the design and operational principles discussed in Chap. 4, the reader may recognize some of the anti-principles as anti-patterns described in the literature on software design. Here, we use the term *anti-principle* rather than *anti-pattern* to emphasize that these general concepts are also valid outside the area of software design.

## 7.2 Past Fragility to Downtime

We apply the anti-principles to study past downtime incidents in Norwegian telecom systems. The major stakeholders did not predict the coincidences that resulted in the outages. Instead, the outages were analyzed by the stakeholders after the fact.

Since knowing the impact of an incident influences how the incident is assessed, it is necessary to be careful when stating the results of a study. Humans have a tendency to concoct explanations for events after they have occurred, making them seem less surprising and more predictable than they really were. This hindsight bias misleads stakeholders into simplifying the causes of an accident, highlighting a single element as the cause and potentially overlooking multiple contributing factors [6, 9, 17, 18, 36].

First, we consider the anti-principle of *uniqueness*. Mobile phone networks are essentially unique infrastructures because the users of one network cannot generally connect to another network when their network experiences problems. If an entire network goes down, millions of mobile phones become useless as communication devices. The largest mobile phone network in Norway went down for about 11 h on June 10, 2011 [65, 66]. The restart of a central node with upgraded software initiated a signal storm that exceeded the network's signalling capacity. The outage affected nearly 3 million customers, or approximately 60 % of all Norwegians. According to top management, the incident was not supposed to happen because earlier restarts of the same node had not caused any problems. The management's surprise and the rare, highly negative outcome of a common operation qualify the signal storm as a black swan incident, at least to top management.

On June 17, 2011, parts of the same mobile phone network went down again due to a new signal storm [67, 68]. According to the Norwegian Post and Telecommunications Authority (NPTA), both signal storms were caused by insufficiently understood dependencies between central nodes in the network combined with insufficient capacity to handle the increasing signal traffic from the many new smartphones. The difficulty in pinpointing the causes of the extreme behavior became evident when, more than a month later, careful technical analyses of the events finally revealed that the signal storms were primarily due to a programming error and not insufficient signal capacity to serve new smartphones [69]. However, the network owner also discussed the need to change the system design and to increase the signal traffic capacity.

The network owner's difficulty in determining the causes of the downtime illustrates that the mobile phone network is indeed a complex adaptive system prone to surprising global behavior. The NPTA publicly stated that the owner needed to improve the network's risk management. While better risk management can assess and mitigate more incidents, perhaps providing longer periods of stable network operation, large-impact incidents will still occur because the network has too many dynamic interactions for humans to reliably foresee rare and extreme behavior. The fundamental problem is not bad risk management but that the four design principles, especially the principles of modularity and weak links, were not fully adhered to when the system was created. Hence, a major outage affecting many customers was bound to happen sooner or later due to the system's uniqueness.

Second, we consider the anti-principle of *connectedness*. All mobile phone networks in Norway are connected to the national power grid. The normal operation of each network depends on a nearly continuous supply of electricity. In late December 2011, the networks went down in a large area of Norway when a storm with hurricane-force winds damaged many power lines, leaving more than 700 base stations belonging to the different networks without electrical power [70]. While the base stations had backup batteries, most lasted a maximum of only four hours. Because landline phone and fixed Internet access were also disrupted in the same area, most people were without communication capabilities following the storm. Although both the power and phone companies worked hard to repair the extensive damage, it took more than a week to restore services to all customers. The problem in 2011 was that the telecom systems were too dependent on the power grid, that is, the telecom system and the power grid were strongly connected systems.

Third, we consider the anti-principle of being *closed*. The telecom networks' strong dependence on the nearly continuous delivery of electrical power came as a surprise to leading Norwegian politicians. Their initial response was to severely criticize the mobile phone companies. According to the NPTA's director general, the people of Norway had come to depend more on the mobile phone systems than the agency had realized before the storm. The fact that both leading politicians and the NPTA were surprised indicates that the consequences of the telecom systems' strong dependencies on the power grid were not fully understood. It is reasonable to suspect that this surprise was due to insufficient information sharing between the network owners and the NPTA, obscuring the fragility to downtime.

The Norwegian Directorate for Civil Protection reports that Norway's largest network owner does not provide major stakeholders, including the Directorate itself, with enough information about changes in the telecom infrastructure [71]. It seems that the owner makes major changes to its infrastructure without informing important stakeholders such as the Norwegian Public Roads Administration, the National Air Navigation service, or the police. Therefore, it has been hard for these institutions to determine the level of exposure they face by using the telecom infrastructure. More publicly available information is needed to discuss and understand the real dangers associated with the use of the telecom infrastructures.

The discussed incidents show that the Norwegian telecom systems were fragile to downtime in 2011 due to the anti-principles of *uniqueness*, *connectedness*, and, most likely, being *closed*.

## 7.3  Indicators of Fragility to Future Downtime

We now turn our attention to properties of telecom infrastructures that indicate fragility to future outages. First, consider the building blocks of the single generic telecom infrastructure in Fig. 7.1 [72]. While the model is quite coarse, it is adequate for our purpose. The model contains one *transport network* and multiple *access networks* [71]. The transport network is the backbone of the telecom infrastructure and moves data over long distances. The access networks give users access to the infrastructure. Some of the access networks consist of one or a few base stations, serving wireless terminals in the vicinity, while others consist of local broadband networks, connecting, for example, homes and offices.

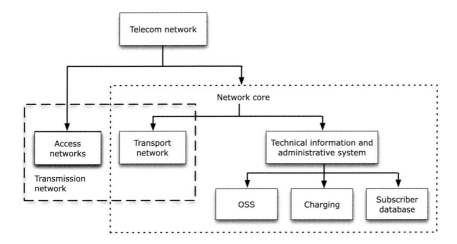

**Fig. 7.1** Hierarchy of networks and systems in a generic telecom infrastructure

Entities owning and operating a transport network and/or access networks are called operators. These operators each have a technical information and administrative system consisting of three smaller systems. Together with the transport network, the three systems constitute the network core. The operations support system (OSS) in Fig. 7.1 configures and provisions the core network nodes. Factors impacting the configuration are the number of subscribers, peak hour call rates, the nature of the services, and geographical preferences. The OSS system also collects network statistics, monitors alarms, and logs various actions of network nodes. The subscriber database contains information on all customers and the charging system calculates the costs chargeable to the customers. Because the subsystems in the network core are needed to set up and take down all user communications, we arrive at the following conclusion:

- A unique technical information and administrative system in the network core indicates fragility to future downtime.

From Sect. 2.7, a system $\mathcal{X}$ depends on a system $\mathcal{Y}$ if a failure in $\mathcal{Y}$ negatively affects the functionality of $\mathcal{X}$. The details of the dependencies between different telecom infrastructures are generally unknown to analysts without close ties to operators, but the main dependencies between access and transport operators are usually known. Figure 7.2 depicts publicly known dependencies between Norwegian operators early in 2014 [72]. The arrows show the direction of these high-level dependencies.

Two systems are *interdependent* when each is dependent on the other. There are interdependencies between the three transport operators in Fig. 7.2. Dependent and interdependent infrastructures allow cascading failures to pass infrastructure boundaries [6]. Figure 7.2 illustrates that it is important to prevent a failure in a single infrastructure from spreading to other infrastructures. Furthermore, since most of the dependency paths in the figure end up in the transport network of the largest operator

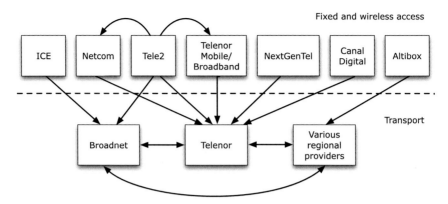

**Fig. 7.2** Access and transport operators in Norway. The *arrows* show the dependencies between the operators. There are interdependencies between the transport operators

(Telenor), fragility to downtime in this transport network is especially serious. If the transport network has an outage, then the outage will spread to nearly all other infrastructures. We therefore note the following:

- A unique transport network connecting multiple operators signals fragility to downtime.

To illustrate the fragility of transport networks, we consider the transport network of Norway's largest operator. While the network's full topology is not publicly known, it includes "self-healing" rings. Figure 7.3 shows a particularly simple ring with two transmission paths between network nodes. If there is a break in one line, the other line may still be available, providing the second is not in close proximity to the first and also damaged. For best protection against failure, different physical routes are used for the two lines. All data are transmitted on the working or active line, while the protection line is on standby. When the active line fails, the two network nodes affected immediately switch to the protection line.

Even a self-healing ring fails, however. On May 23, 2011, both transmission lines of a ring in the largest operator's transmission network failed [73]. Due to roadwork, one line was temporarily moved aboveground by installing a temporary cable. An excavator broke this cable by accident. About seven minutes later, a falling tree cut the other line somewhere else in the country, causing an outage affecting mobile phone customers in large parts of Norway for about three and a half hours. Air traffic

**Fig. 7.3** Conceptual
self-healing ring

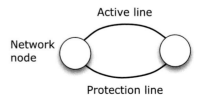

was also affected because a regional flight control center lost its phone connections. The incident shows that having only two cables transporting the major part of the telecom traffic between different geographical parts of a country is unsafe, especially when both cables are aboveground.

## 7.4  Robust Access Networks

Using the above understanding of fragility to downtime in telecom infrastructures, we now consider how to make future infrastructures robust to downtime. The expected seamless integration of Wi-Fi and mobile network technologies and the emerging Internet of Things will lead to a massive increase in the number of mobile and stationary devices connecting wirelessly to telecom networks. Many believe that machine-to-machine communications supporting smart grids, smart homes and cities, and electronic health will be particularly important. All the new devices and new data-hungry services will lead to a huge increase in wireless data traffic. Examples of devices are notebooks, mobile phones, tablets, televisions, kitchen appliances, smartwatches, 3D glasses, drones, robots, sensors, and actuators, while examples of services involve high-definition video available anywhere, continuous real-time interactions between individuals, and medical sensors monitoring people's health.

To fulfill future communication needs in a power- and frequency-efficient manner, the deployment of multiple layers of radio coverage is most likely necessary where traditional macrocell towers provide a blanket of coverage while, under the blanket, thousands of small cells provide high data rates in areas such as malls, airports, arenas, public plazas, urban parks, and business districts [63]. Because most devices will be close to base stations, it is possible to provide high data rates while keeping the signal power low. The use of small low-power cells enables the increased reuse of frequencies across cells. Today's national telecom infrastructure with many access networks already has thousands of expensive base stations. In fact, the base stations constitute a large percentage of the total cost of current telecom networks. One attractive possibility to limit the costs of even more base stations is to move much of the stations' functionality to the cloud.

High-speed links between the base stations and the cloud are needed to satisfy the stringent delay requirements enabling radio signal processing in the cloud. Data from multiple base stations can be used to alleviate the increased multi-cell interference due to reduced cell size by dynamically adjusting the radio signaling according to channel conditions. To further limit processing delays, use of a highly distributed cloud architecture with local access network clouds is possible, as depicted in Fig. 7.4, where each access network cloud consists of a cluster of commodity and special-purpose hardware. Hence, the access networks will become much more intelligent than they are today.

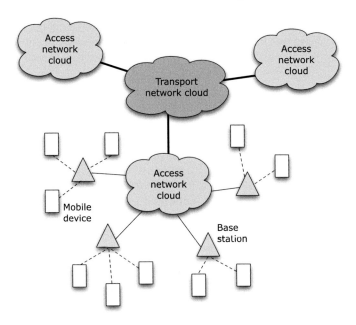

**Fig. 7.4**  Possible architecture of cloud-based telecom infrastructure

Flexibility in how much processing is done in the access network clouds is needed to support varying types of services and link delays. The upper layers of the base stations' radio protocol stack can most easily be moved to the cloud, such as admission/congestion control and radio resource management algorithms. If low-delay links are available, then lower-layer functions, for example, parts of the physical and medium access control layers, can also be moved to the cloud [63, 64].

By moving most of the base stations' functionality from the cell sites to access network clouds, a provider no longer needs to build enough processing capacity into every base station to handle peak traffic conditions [63, 64]. Instead, the provider can allocate processing resources to the parts of the access networks where they are most needed at any given time. For example, in the evening hours, the processing resources can be adjusted according to shifting service demands as phone users move from a city's business district and to its suburbs.

When there are low-delay links between the base stations and the clouds, each base station is reduced to a radio and an antenna array. While today's access networks are costly and time-consuming to upgrade, future generations of access networks would simply be software upgrades in the cloud. Using the four design principles of modules, weak links, redundancy, and diversity together with the implementation ideas introduced by Netflix, it is possible to develop cloud-based implementations of base station functionality that are robust to downtime. Cloud implementations will isolate local failures to break any positive feedback loops, as discussed in Chap. 5.

## 7.5 Robust Network Core

There are at least three ways to make a network core (see Fig. 7.1) robust to unplanned downtime. First, telecom operators should realize the functionality of nodes in the network core in a transport network cloud, as shown in Fig. 7.4. Again, the design principles of modules, weak links, redundancy, and diversity make it possible to isolate local failures. Furthermore, cloud implementation allows operators to upgrade software without taking down and restarting nodes. This advantage is important, since it takes a long time to restart central nodes in today's systems. The cloud also increases the programmability and controllability of the network core because good development and monitoring tools exist for the cloud. Operators may use a private cloud to control its hardware layer. To reduce costs, several operators could share a community cloud infrastructure.

Second, to reduce the chance of a major outage, operators should improve the redundancy of the transmission paths in their transport networks. A risk analysis [74] from 2012 of the largest transport network in Norway recommends additional redundant paths to avoid incidents similar to the outage of May 23, 2011, described at the end of Sect. 7.3.

Third, to make it harder for local failures to spread, operators could deploy equipment from different vendors to increase the hardware and software diversity of the nodes in the network core [72]. However, the advantage of added vendor diversity must be weighed against the extra resources needed to operate and maintain a diverse system. In particular, the use of equipment from different vendors could lead to compatibility issues.

## 7.6 Reduced Dependency on the Power Grid

The December storm discussed in the second half of Sect. 7.2 revealed the Norwegian telecom infrastructures' strong dependence on the national power grid [70]. Strong winds damaged many power lines, causing more than 700 base stations to go down after their backup batteries were quickly depleted. To reduce the dependency on a nearly continuous supply of electricity, the NPTA required network operators to improve their backup power solutions to ensure that the 1,000 base stations covering the most critical areas of Norway have backup power for at least 72 h [70]. All other base stations were required to have at least six hours of backup power. In addition, the operators were told to prepare more resources and develop better contingency plans to enable local crews to quickly repair damaged power lines and base stations.

## 7.7  Reduced Dependency on One Infrastructure

In general, a unique complex system should not implement a service of critical national importance when the impact of a black or gray swan is intolerable [7]. The impact of extreme global behavior is reduced by realizing a critically important service using two different systems. It is vital that a failure in one system does not cause a failure in the other. It is not sufficient to deploy two identical systems because they obviously have common vulnerabilities; the systems must have diverse designs or implementations. Of course, simultaneously targeted attacks can still bring down both systems, but diversity is likely to make such attacks costly and difficult to successfully carry out.

After the 2011 outages discussed earlier, customers wondered why they were not switched to another network when their home network went down. The simple answer is that none of the networks had the capacity to service a huge number of additional users. The network infrastructure needed large and expensive changes to facilitate such a switch. However, it is economically viable to give a limited group of people with important responsibilities during a crisis access to several operators' networks, either by giving them phones with multiple subscriber identity module (SIM) cards or by adding functionality to switch the group members between networks.

To further reduce the impact of outages in commercial telecom networks, emergency services in Norway have their own telecom network, called the Norwegian Public Safety Network. This network covers all populated areas of Norway. While current commercial networks are based on the same technology (LTE), the emergency network is based on another technology (TETRA), especially developed for emergency communication. None of its roughly 2,000 base stations have less than eight hours of backup power and 15 % of the stations have 48 h worth (http://dinkom. no/en). The emergency network only supports low-speed data communication.

## 7.8  Anti-fragility to Downtime

While implementations of the four design principles make cloud-based telecom infrastructures robust to downtime, the operational principle must be implemented to make the systems anti-fragile to downtime, that is, robustness must be maintained over time by learning from small incidents.

The stakeholders of telecom infrastructures may balk at the idea of deliberately introducing failures to quickly detect vulnerabilities. Granted, it may be a bad idea to induce failures in today's infrastructures. However, if a telecom infrastructure is designed and implemented in the cloud according to the four design principles, then it should be possible to induce local failures without creating a significant danger of systemic failure causing prolonged downtime. Cloud implementation then makes it possible to quickly discover vulnerabilities in administrative systems, in nodes in the network core, and in the base station functionality.

When infrastructures are able to confine the impact of local failures, operators can constantly adjust their systems to keep them within the bounds of normal operations. The adjustments involve tinkering with selected parts and processes of the systems. Not all tinkering will have the desired effect, because it is hard to foresee the consequences of changes to complex systems, especially large telecom infrastructures. To react quickly to unusual behavior, it is necessary to monitor an infrastructure. It is not enough to just monitor each part of the infrastructure. Because a system's complexity first and foremost stems from the many interactions between its parts, a global view of the system's behavior is necessary. A system must be monitored at all times, especially when it experiences problems.

Because failures will occur in complex systems no matter how many resources are used on high-quality risk analysis, reactive measurements are needed to limit the impact of surprising incidents. In practice, there is a trade-off between proactive and reactive measures to reduce downtime. A risk analysis [74] of Norwegian telecom networks using Internet protocol version 4 (IPv4) suggests that sometimes it is better to improve operations, maintenance, and the ability to quickly react to problems than to make specific parts of the incumbent network infrastructure more robust to downtime. These actions will benefit all Norwegian providers (see Fig. 7.2), while physical changes will mostly provide local or regional benefits.

## 7.9 Discussion and Summary

Although we do not have any general method to measure an information and communications technology (ICT) system's degree of anti-fragility to downtime, it is possible to determine when a system is fragile to outages. Here, we applied three anti-principles to determine fragilities to downtime. These anti-principles were selected because they proved useful during the investigation. While we have only applied the anti-principles to telecom systems in Norway, it is not hard to apply them to other types of ICT systems. Experience with anti-principles indicates that many systems are fragile to downtime. Many more anti-principles exist (http://sourcemaking.com). Additional work is needed to determine other anti-principles that reveal fragility in ICT systems.

We should move as much functionality of a telecom infrastructure as possible to the cloud and apply the five design and operational principles to create anti-fragility to downtime. A service-oriented architecture (SOA) with microservices is most likely a good way to achieve anti-fragility in practice. There is no need to use public cloud infrastructures. A better solution is to use private, specialized clouds with, perhaps, custom hardware for signal processing, in addition to commodity hardware. The important point is that the amount of custom hardware can be reduced significantly compared to today's telecom systems.

Due the diverse expertise and huge amount of work required, it is outside the scope of this book to determine and analyze all aspects of telecom systems leading to fragility to downtime. In particular, we mention the need to study the protocols

of telecom systems. Future systems are likely to use IPv6, which has known vulnerabilities, including fragility to denial-of-service attacks denying regular customers
access to telecom services. The creation of anti-fragile protocols is an interesting
research topic.

---

**What to learn from Part II**

Part II has studied the fragility, robustness, and anti-fragility of Netflix's media
streaming solution, the Norwegian e-government system Altinn, and Norway's
telecom infrastructure. The case studies provide strong evidence that careful
application of the five design and operational principles introduced in Chap. 4
can provide anti-fragility to downtime, that is, the principles lead to systems
with less downtime than today's strongly connected, highly optimized systems
with little ability to handle unforeseen events. Furthermore, the cloud facilitates
the realization of these principles, although the principles are also believed to be
valid for non-cloud systems. While the five principles are easy to understand at
an abstract level, the case studies demonstrate that the challenge is to determine
how to implement the principles in real systems.

Anti-fragile software solutions in the cloud should be based on SOA with
microservices, preferably implemented and operated by development and operations (DevOps) teams with "skin in the game." SOA and microservices together
model a software solution as a set of independently deployable and scalable
services with well-defined interfaces. This architecture style supports the development and management of services by multiple, largely independent teams
using different programming languages, continuous deployment, and highly
redundant and scalable data storage. The use of microservices with limited functionality makes it possible to ensure the graceful degradation of an application's
functionality. Each service's limited functionality facilitates the development of
automated fallback responses in the case of local failures. When a local failure affects a service, other services depending on this malfunctioning service
receive a standardized response.

---

# Part III
# Anti-fragility to Malware

# Chapter 8
# Robustness to Malware Spreading

While many networked computing systems are vulnerable to self-propagating malicious software, or malware, large enterprises use automated patching and hardening to make their systems highly immune to malware infections. Still, persistent human attackers compromise enterprise networks utilizing advanced tools, customized malware, and zero-day exploits that anti-malware technology and patching cannot detect and mitigate [75, 76]. The three chapters in Part III study how the diversity and fail fast principles from Chap. 4 can be exploited to achieve antifragility to malware spreading in networked systems. The current chapter investigates software diversity's ability to make systems robust to the spreading of infectious malware and argues that diversity increases the time needed to compromise enterprise systems, thus increasing the probability of early detection and mitigation. The two next chapters extend the results in this chapter to achieve anti-fragility to malware spreading.

## 8.1 Introduction

We view a computing system as a collection of interconnected computing devices and consider the devices at the operating system (OS) and application levels. Compilers with "diversity engines" generate the devices' binary images, producing many different executable images from a much smaller set of OS and application source codes [24]. Many techniques to diversify binary images exist [77]. A transformation can be as simple as adding no-operation instructions (NOPs) to an image. The insertion of NOPs is always possible and allows us to produce infinitely many binary variants. Conceptually, a program's binary images are divided into classes such that all members of the same class share at least one exploitable vulnerability, while members of different classes have no common exploitable vulnerabilities. Assuming that the classes are roughly equally large, the number of classes measures the program's diversity with the convention that a network with only a single type, that is, a software monoculture, has no diversity [50].

© The Author(s) 2016                                                                 81
K.J. Hole, *Anti-fragile ICT Systems*, Simula SpringerBriefs on Computing 1,
DOI 10.1007/978-3-319-30070-2_8

Using well-established network models from network science [23], we combine software diversity and computer "immunization" to halt multiple simultaneous outbreaks of infectious malware with sparse and inhomogeneous spreading patterns, represented by synthetic and empirical networks. We establish an explanatory epidemiological model of variable diversity, determine a general lower bound on the diversity needed, evaluate the halting technique's performance for worst-case spreading over sparse and dense homogeneous networks, consider diversity's ability to slow down persistent threats, and discuss independent research on software diversity.

This chapter proposes and analyzes a halting technique for malware with known static spreading mechanisms. The technique assumes that a small percentage of the nodes can be immunized, that is, made resistant to the malware. In practice, immunization, or hardening, includes the removal of non-essential software programs, the secure configuration of remaining programs, constant patching, and the use of firewalls and intrusion prevention systems. The author first presented the halting technique in [56]. Chapter 10 generalizes the halting technique to malware with unknown and time-varying spreading mechanisms.

## 8.2  Explanatory Epidemiological Model

Different malware strains exploit vulnerabilities in OSs and application software to infect computing devices. An exploitable vulnerability is a mistake in the software that enables malware to gain access to a device and its information. Examples of exploitable vulnerabilities are buffer overflows and malformed URLs (see [24, 78, 79] for more information on vulnerabilities). Infectious malware can spread to new vulnerable devices via network shares, removable media, Internet protocol (IP) attacks, email messages, instant messaging, and peer-to-peer networks.

### 8.2.1  Epidemiological Model

We model the spreading of infectious malware over networked computing devices by a simple graph (no self-loops or parallel edges) with $N$ nodes of $L$ types, $1 \leq L \leq N$, as depicted in Fig. 8.1. There are roughly $N/L$ nodes of each type uniformly distributed over the graph. The node types represent different binary codes at the OS or application level of the computing devices; that is, nodes of the same type share an exploitable vulnerability while nodes of different types have no common exploitable vulnerabilities. The edges represent communications between nodes. A good measure of the model's *diversity* is the number of node types $L$ (see [50] for a thorough discussion of diversity). Two nodes are neighbors if they share an edge. A node's degree $k$ is the number of neighbors and $\langle k \rangle$ denotes the nodes' average degree. A network is *homogeneous* when all nodes have degrees $k \approx \langle k \rangle$ and *inhomogeneous* when a small fraction of nodes, called *hubs*, have $k \gg \langle k \rangle$.

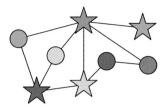

**Fig. 8.1** A network with $N = 8$ nodes, $L = 4$ node types of different colors, and average degree $\langle k \rangle = 2.5$. *Stars* represent the infected seeds. There is $S = 1$ seed per node type. Only the *orange* seed will infect a neighbor

The malware's different spreading mechanisms determine the topologies of the spreading networks. Malware utilizing random scanning to target IP addresses spread over nearly fully connected homogeneous networks, while malware utilizing topological scanning travel over inhomogeneous networks [80]. Topological scanning relies on information contained in infected hosts to locate new targets, including routing tables, email addresses, and Uniform Resource Locators (URLs). The resulting virtual spreading networks are different from the physical networks of wired and wireless communication links. We study multiple malware, or *multimalware*, outbreaks because the deployment of several malware types is an obvious strategy to counter software diversity. All malware types are assumed to have the same spreading mechanism.

Our discrete-time model contains $L$ types of infectious malware, that is, one malware type per node type. Each malware type exploits a particular vulnerability to infect a single node type. Initially, $S$ nodes of each type are infected. These $L \cdot S$ nodes are called *seeds* (see Fig. 8.1). The infection probability determines the rate at which a sick node infects a susceptible neighbor of the same type during a time step. To study worst-case spreading, we set the infection probability to one to ensure that all nodes reachable from the seeds are infected. No infected node recovers.

## 8.2.2 Non-predictive Model

It is hard to estimate the actual spreading of malware in a networked computing system because it is influenced by many factors, including router policies, the choice of communication protocols, available bandwidth, traffic loads, firewall rules, anti-malware signature sets, intrusion detection, the level of software patching, and the misconfiguration of system parts. Rather than trying to incorporate all these factors, the epidemiological model displays very fast worst-case spreading where an infectious node always infects all of its neighbors of the same type. While this model cannot predict actual spreading in a network, it can explain the usefulness of software diversity. Because actual malware is likely to spread less, it is reasonable to believe that the model's malware halting translates into malware halting in real systems. This view is supported by independent research discussed later in the chapter.

## 8.3  Malware-Halting Technique

The following proposed malware-halting technique immunizes hubs if they exist and increases the diversity $L$ to limit the fraction of infected nodes:

1. If the spreading network is inhomogeneous, immunize enough large-degree nodes to create a homogeneous subnet when the immunized nodes and their adjacent edges are removed.
2. Ensure that the node diversity of the homogeneous subnet is large enough to halt multiple simultaneous malware outbreaks.

Table 8.1 outlines how to halt multimalware outbreaks on sparse (small $\langle k \rangle$) or dense (large $\langle k \rangle$) networks with homogeneous or inhomogeneous topologies. Limited *true* diversity (small $L$) is obtained by deploying instances of different OSs and applications with similar functionality. Michael Franz [24] argues that much greater *artificial* diversity (large $L$) is available when users download software from application stores utilizing compiler-generated diversity to produce many classes of executable binary images. While true diversity is costly because the installation of different software forces users to learn new functionality, the cost of artificial diversity is reasonable, since the functionality is not changed.

An example illustrates the halting technique on a sparse and inhomogeneous network with hubs. Figure 8.2a shows a synthetic network with 300 nodes. The nodes are circles with areas proportional to their degrees, thus highlighting the hubs. The spreading network is a software monoculture with one node type ($L = 1$) [28, 29]. All nodes are red to illustrate that a single seed ($S = 1$) infects all nodes. Figure 8.2b shows the same network, but now with randomly distributed orange and yellow node types ($L = 2$). Eight white hubs are made immune to two malware types attacking the nodes. There is little malware spreading in this immunized "polyculture." For a particular selection of two seeds of different types, Fig. 8.2b shows that the malware spreading is reduced from 300 nodes to only three red nodes; that is, the halting technique decreases the percentage of infected nodes from 100 to 1 %.

The simple illustrative spreading network in Fig. 8.2 has no loops and the hubs are connected in a small subnetwork. During the following analysis, we consider networks with loops and make no assumptions about how the hubs are connected.

**Table 8.1** Malware halting on spreading networks with different topologies

| Malware halting on different network topologies | | |
|---|---|---|
| Sparse and homogeneous | Sparse and inhomogeneous | Dense and homogeneous |
| Utilize small true or artificial diversity | Use hub immunization and small true or artificial diversity | Deploy large artificial diversity |

**Fig. 8.2  a** Monoculture
with 300 infected nodes
whose areas are proportional
to their edge degrees. **b** The
same network as in (**a**) but
with *white* immunized hubs
and *orange* and *yellow* node
types. Two malware types,
each with a single randomly
selected seed, only manage
to infect one additional node

**(a)**

**(b)**

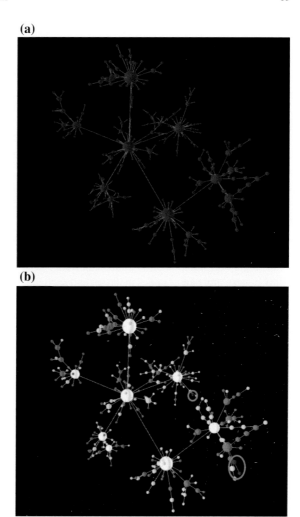

## 8.4  Halting Technique Analysis

The epidemiological model represents the spreading phase of multimalware outbreaks. The following approximate analysis of this phase establishes a lower bound
on the diversity $L$ needed by the halting technique summarized by Table 8.1.

We first clarify why hubs should be immunized in an inhomogeneous spreading
network. When the infection probability is *small* and the malware spreading origi-
nates from a *single* randomly selected seed, a strategically placed node in the "core"
of a monoculture contributes more to the spreading than a hub on the network's
periphery does [81]. However, we study polycultures with a *maximum* infection
probability equal to one and *multiple* widespread seeds per node type. Consider a

hub with a large degree $D$ on the periphery of a network. Since the $S$ seeds with the same type as the hub are uniformly distributed over the network, one of the hub's neighbors could be a seed. When this seed infects the hub, the hub will again infect roughly $D/L$ of its neighbors of the same type. We want to prevent this peripheral hub infection because $D$ tends to be much larger than $L$ and because any of the $D/L$ infectious nodes can cause extensive malware spreading when the infection probability is one.

Since different malware spreading mechanisms result in distinct spreading patterns, it is essential to analyze malware outbreaks on spreading networks with arbitrary degree distributions. Let the nodes in a network be numbered from one to $N$ and let node $i$ have degree $k_i$, $i = 1, \ldots, N$. We consider the ensemble of random networks with an arbitrary but fixed degree sequence $\{k_i\}$ generated by the so-called configuration model (see [23, Sect. 13.2] for details). All networks have a mean degree $\langle k \rangle = 1/N \sum_i k_i$ and a mean-squared degree $\langle k^2 \rangle = 1/N \sum_i k_i^2$. Any network has $L$ node types, with (approximately) $N/L$ nodes of each type.

A *single-type component* is a subset of nodes of the same type such that there is a path between any pair of nodes in the set and such that it is not possible to add another node of the same type to the set while preserving this property. The two orange nodes in Fig. 8.1 constitute the largest single-type component. A single-type component is a *giant component* when its size is proportional to $N/L$. If a single-type component contains a seed, then all its nodes will be infected.

We study single-type components in a network to limit the overall fraction of infected nodes. Let this fraction be averaged over many model runs, where each run has $L \cdot S$ randomly selected seeds. The underlying network topology is the same for all malware types, since they are assumed to have the same spreading mechanism and the nodes of different types are uniformly distributed over the network. A particular malware type only infects a single type of nodes. Hence, malware of different types infects distinct subsets of nodes. Because each subset has $N/L$ nodes, all subsets have the same fraction of infected nodes when averaged over many model runs. Consequently, the average fraction of infected nodes over all types can be analyzed by considering a *monoculture subgraph*, defined by all the nodes of an arbitrary but fixed type and the edges connecting these nodes. All other nodes and their adjacent edges can be ignored.

To limit the average fraction of infected nodes, we want to choose the diversity $L$ such that the monoculture subgraph does not have a giant component. This subgraph has a mean degree $\langle k \rangle/L$ and a mean-squared degree $\langle k^2 \rangle/L^2$ for large $N$. Because the subgraph is contained in a random network generated by the configuration model, the subgraph has a giant component if and only if $\langle k^2 \rangle/L^2 > 2\langle k \rangle/L$ in the limit for large $N$ [23, p. 456]. To prevent the formation of a giant component, we need $\langle k^2 \rangle/L \leq 2\langle k \rangle$ or, equivalently, we choose the diversity $L$ such that

$$L \geq \left\lceil \frac{\langle k^2 \rangle}{2\langle k \rangle} \right\rceil. \tag{8.1}$$

The right-hand side of inequality (8.1) is large for inhomogeneous networks because $k_i^2$ is much larger than $k_i$ for hubs. However, hub immunization reduces the lower bound. When the nodes with the largest degrees in the original network are immunized, we obtain a new network with $N' < N$ susceptible nodes and smaller node degrees $d_j$, $j = 1, \ldots, N'$. The new network is obtained by ignoring all immunized hubs and their adjacent edges because they no longer contribute to malware spreading. This network "pruning" affects the previously discussed mono-culture subgraph. The new mean-squared degree $\langle d^2 \rangle = 1/N' \sum_j d_j^2$ and mean degree $\langle d \rangle = 1/N' \sum_j d_j$ should be substituted for $\langle k^2 \rangle$ and $\langle k \rangle$ in inequality (8.1) to determine the minimum needed diversity $L$.

Whether or not hubs in the original network are immunized to obtain a new network, the $S$ seeds in a monoculture subgraph can spread over at most $S$ components of this subgraph. These components are small in graphs without a giant component [23], leading to a small fraction of infected nodes. Inequality (8.1) shows a trade-off between the required number of node types $L$ and the number of immunized hubs. If it is possible to generate many node types, then the fraction of immunized hubs can be reduced, making it possible to halt malware outbreaks on very large inhomogeneous networks.

## 8.5   Halting Technique Performance

We have seen that the hubs in a spreading network with inhomogeneous topology can be immunized to obtain a homogeneous network. If the hubs are not known, then acquaintance immunization can be used to protect most hubs [25]. Acquaintance immunization will be discussed in Chap. 9. Here, we apply the malware-halting technique to synthetic and empirical spreading networks with homogeneous topologies. Each network represents the worst-case spreading of $S$ malware outbreaks per node type. While inequality (8.1) is only strictly valid for random networks in the limit of large $N$, the following NetLogo [46] simulations show that the lower bound determines the needed diversity.

### 8.5.1   Sparse and Homogeneous Networks

Wireless devices, particularly smartphones, can communicate via short-range wireless links such as Wi-Fi and Bluetooth links. In our first epidemiological simulations, different malware types copy themselves to new devices by opening wireless connections. Sparse and homogeneous proximity networks represent the spreading patterns. The NetLogo model generates a proximity network with an average node degree $\langle k \rangle$ by first placing $N$ nodes uniformly at random on a square. An edge is then added between a randomly chosen node and its closest neighbor in Euclidean distance.

**Table 8.2** The minimum number of node types needed to halt malware outbreaks on homogeneous proximity networks with 5,000 nodes and an increasing average node degree

| Proximity networks | | | | |
|---|---|---|---|---|
| Average node degree $\langle k \rangle$ | 5 | 6 | 7 | 8 |
| Minimum needed node types $L$ | 3 | 4 | 4 | 5 |
| Fraction of infected nodes | 3.4 % | 3.6 % | 4.6 % | 4.8 % |

Each fraction of infected nodes is averaged over 500 networks with uniform random distribution of node types and seeds

More edges are similarly added until the network has the desired average degree $\langle k \rangle$. Self-loops and multiple edges between nodes are not allowed. Note that although handheld devices move over time, we only model short-term malware spreading assuming static networks. Wireless sensor networks stay fixed for long periods.

Table 8.2 lists the lower bounds on the needed diversity $L$, obtained from inequality (8.1), for proximity networks with 5,000 nodes and an increasing average degree $\langle k \rangle$. Each fraction of infected nodes is averaged over 500 networks with the same average degree and uniform distribution of node types, including $S = 10$ seeds per type. Only connected networks were evaluated, that is, networks with isolated subgraphs were ignored. The lower bound on the diversity $L$ was the same for all evaluated networks with a given average degree.

While the deterministic epidemiological model causes all nodes to become infected in a monoculture ($L = 1$), less than 5 % of the nodes became infected in the diverse proximity networks, according to Table 8.2. Previously published simulation results and mathematical analyses of other network models confirm that small true or artificial diversity is sufficient to halt multimalware outbreaks on homogeneous and sparse networks [82].

We also analyze malware halting on a sparse network where the nodes represent email addresses and the links represent e-mail exchanges between the addresses. The network has 1,133 nodes and 5,451 edges. The largest node has degree 71 and the average degree is 9.62. While the network is slightly inhomogeneous, we forgo the immunization of large-degree nodes. The lower bound on the diversity is $L \geq 10$. Since the network is small, we assume only $S = 1$ seed per node type.

Ignoring the fact that email malware needs help from unknowing users to propagate, the simulations determined the fraction of infected nodes averaged over 5,000 random configurations of node types and seeds for increasing diversity $L = 10, 11, \ldots, 16$. The fraction of infected nodes decreases from 8 to 4 % when the diversity increases from 10 to 16. The additional decrease in the fraction of infected nodes is relatively small for diversity above the lower bound in inequality (8.1). Earlier reported simulation results for other networks [82] show similar modest reductions in the fraction of infected nodes for diversities beyond the minimum required value.

### 8.5.2 Dense and Homogeneous Networks

Consider the case where $L$ types of random scanning malware spread over a complete network with $N$ nodes of degree $k = N - 1$. There are $L$ node types and $N/L$ nodes per type. The types are uniformly distributed over the nodes of the network. Assume one seed per node type. Each seed has edges to the other $N/L - 1$ nodes of the same type. Together, the $N/L$ single-type nodes form a star graph with the seed in the center. Since the seed will always infect all the peripheral nodes in the star graph, it does not help to increase the number of node types $L$ as long as there is one seed per node type. All $N$ nodes will still be infected. The only way to halt multimalware outbreaks is to use many more nodes types than there are malware types.

If there are $M$ malware types, then $M \cdot N/L$ nodes will be infected. Hence, the diversity $L$ needs to be proportional to $N$ and the number of malware types $M$ must be much smaller than $N$ to prevent a large infection. This observation is in accordance with the diversity bound in inequality (8.1), which is equal to $L \geq (N - 1)/2$ for $k = N - 1$. More generally, consider an arbitrary path consisting of $m$ edges in a dense network. The path's nodes are all of the same type with probability $L^{-m}$ for $m \leq N/L$. We must have diversity $L \approx N$ to ensure that this probability is very small even for very short paths. As stated in Table 8.1, large artificial diversity is needed to halt malware spreading over homogeneous dense networks with many nodes.

Since it is not completely clear how much artificial diversity is obtainable with compilers utilizing diversification techniques [24], we cannot conclude that the halting technique is applicable to multimalware outbreaks with *dense* spreading patterns. However, Todd Jackson [83] and his colleagues convincingly argue that application stores can produce massive-scale software diversity. Furthermore, as we transition from Internet protocol version 4 (IPv4) to IPv6, topological scanning may become more popular than random scanning due to the huge number of unused IPv6 addresses.

## 8.6 Persistent Targeted Attacks

The term *advanced persistent threats* refers to attackers employing more or less advanced techniques to first learn about and then compromise selected computer systems without being detected, at least not for a long time [75, 76]. Examples of persistent threats are state-sponsored attacks on foreign commercial and governmental enterprises to steal industrial and military secrets. The attacks are often initiated by well-timed, socially engineered spear-phishing emails delivering trojans to individuals with access to sensitive information. Malicious email is leveraged because most enterprises allow email to enter their networks.

Persistent attackers frequently exploit OS or application vulnerabilities in the targeted systems. An attacker first develops a payload to exploit one or more vulnerabilities. Next, an automated tool such as a PDF or Microsoft document delivers the payload to a few users of a system. The payload installs a backdoor or provides remote system access, allowing the attacker to establish a presence inside the trusted system boundary. Finally, the attacker violates the confidentiality, integrity, or availability of the system to achieve his or her goals.

We shall see that large software diversity increases the time persistent attackers need to compromise systems, thus providing defenders with more time to detect the probing of their system defenses, collect information about the attackers, and deploy countermeasures to prevent major system breaches. As before, we divide the binary files implementing the functionality of a particular program into $L$ roughly equally large classes such that all members of the same class share at least one exploitable vulnerability, while members of different classes have no common exploitable vulnerability. If a user and an attacker download the same program from an application store [24, 83], then the two downloaded files share an exploitable vulnerability with probability $1/L$. When the diversity $L$ is large, the probability of a common vulnerability is small and attackers can no longer reliably analyze their own downloaded program files to exploit vulnerabilities in users' program files. (Note that the diversity $L$ must be large even if the lower bound in inequality (8.1) is small.)

Directed attacks against specific computers running known programs become more difficult, as long as the attacker has no way of determining which specific binary is running on what computer. Since it is necessary to create security patches tailored to the different binary versions of the same program [24, 83], it becomes impossible for an attacker to reverse-engineer software patches by comparing a particular patch to the corresponding code on a user's computer because the patch and code are both unknown to the attacker.

## 8.7  Related Work

Miguel Garcia [78] and his colleagues have studied true diversity at the OS level by considering exploitable OS vulnerabilities published over a period of roughly 15 years. The authors carefully analyzed vulnerabilities in 11 different OSs to determine how many of these vulnerabilities occur in more than one OS. More than 50 % of the 55 studied OS pairs have at most one remotely exploitable common vulnerability. The low numbers of shared vulnerabilities for different OS combinations strongly indicate that true diversity is obtainable with off-the-shelf OSs. The authors also provide a good overview of related research on software diversity.

Jin Han [79] and his colleagues have shown that true diversity is available at the application level with off-the-shelf software. The authors analyzed over 6,000 application vulnerabilities published in 2007. About 98.6 % of the studied applications have substitutes, that is, applications that offer similar functionality, and the majority of the applications either do not have the same vulnerability or cannot be compromised with the same exploit code. Nearly half of the applications are officially supported to run on multiple OSs. Although the different OS distributions of the same application are likely to suffer from the same vulnerability, the attack code is different in most cases.

Work by Konstantinos Kravvaritis [84] and his colleagues supports the need for more software diversity in real networked systems. The authors reasonably assume that binary files with the same name are realizations of a single program; that is, the files may be different at the binary level but their functionality is identical. A client–server application collected executable program and library files from individuals who installed the client application on their computers. The client calculated the MD5 hash of each collected file and sent the hash to the server. Since the hash is unique for each different input file, the server could determine whether or not binary files with the same name were identical.

Kravvaritis [84] and his colleagues defined three metrics to measure the diversity of binary files with the same name. One metric, which estimates the probability of a successful targeted attack, is given by $m/n$, where $m$ is the number of instances of the most frequent binary variant of a program and $n$ is the total number of instances. The server collected 1,309,834 binary instances of 205,221 files with different names. For more than half of the files analyzed, the estimated chance of a successful attack is in excess of 50 %. The values of all three metrics indicate that the diversity of current software platforms is too low to significantly slow down targeted attacks. Hence, there is a real need for the large compiler-generated diversity discussed in this chapter.

Research by Pu Wang [85] and colleagues confirms that the number of giant components with nodes of the same type determines the extent to which malware of different types spread over diverse networks. The authors study the calling patterns of 6.2 million mobile phone subscribers to determine possible spreading patterns of malware attacking smartphone OSs. When a smartphone OS's market share is small, there is no giant component of the call network connecting most phones with this OS. Although the call network is connected, a subgraph of smartphones sharing the same OS is fragmented into many small and disjoint components [85]. The lack of large components on which different types of malware can spread explains the low observed saturation of malware in real mobile phone networks. Nevertheless, future malware epidemics are possible because two OS families currently dominate the smartphone market and more and more people buy smartphones.

Juan Caballero [86] and his colleagues have shown that the judicious use of true diversity improves the robustness of the Internet routing infrastructure against software vulnerabilities facilitating denial-of-service attacks, remote execution of system-level commands without authentication, and unauthorized privileged access. While the use of different software implementations from different code bases on different routers increases the network's overall robustness, it also increases the complexity and costs of network deployment and management. Artificial diversity, as suggested by Franz [24], is an interesting alternative to true diversity because the complexity and costs are much reduced.

Graph coloring is the assignment of colors to the nodes in a graph subject to a constraint [86]. Not surprisingly, a good coloring algorithm needs fewer colors to obtain adequate true diversity on a network compared to just distributing colors uniformly over the network devices, as done here. Because the best coloring algorithms necessitate central coordination to install the correct software on the different devices, these algorithms are best suited to slow-changing infrastructures managed by skilled personnel. Coloring algorithms are less useful when general users manage computing devices. The advantage of deploying application stores incorporating compilers with diversity engines is that adequate diversity is achieved with very little involvement from device owners.

## 8.8  Summary

While the Internet's numerous networks are diverse due to distinct configurations, firewall rules, anti-malware signature sets, intrusion detection, and router policies, many networks still have limited internal diversity, making them vulnerable to serious malware spreading. The multimalware-halting technique presented can halt outbreaks on these networks.

Advanced persistent threats represent a serious challenge to defenders of networked systems with very sensitive information. Our analysis shows that software diversity makes it harder to infect computing devices in these systems. Eventually, large-scale experiments will be needed to determine how to best deploy software diversity to make systems more robust to malware.

# Chapter 9
# Robustness to Malware Reinfections

In Chap. 8, we analyzed a deterministic epidemiological model where an infected node immediately contaminated all its neighbors of the same type. The spreading process was completely determined by the spreading network's topology, the configuration of node types, and the selection of initially infected nodes or seeds. Because no node recovered from an infection, there were no long-term dynamics. The spreading simply stopped when all reachable nodes were infected. Here, we study a stochastic epidemiological model of multimalware outbreaks where arbitrary but fixed probabilities determine whether nodes are infected. Furthermore, nodes recover from infections with given probabilities, only to be reinfected later. An incident from 2007, where the same worm repeatedly infected the internal networks of a Norwegian bank, illustrates how reinfections can occur in real networks.

The stochastic epidemiological model is first used to determine how to immunize unknown hubs on diverse inhomogeneous spreading networks. A simple solution is obtained by generalizing the acquaintance immunization strategy for monoculture networks [25]. Next, the model is analyzed to determine the software diversity required to halt multimalware spreading in homogeneous spreading networks where nodes can be infected multiple times by the same malware. The analysis produces a lower bound on the diversity needed to ensure that, with a high probability, the malware outbreaks do not spread far but, instead, die out quickly. The lower bound is obtained by modifying a "classical" result from network science [87]. A reader unfamiliar with differential equations can skip the development of the bound, since it is not needed to understand the remaining chapters.

## 9.1 Malware Attack on a Norwegian Bank

In March 2007, Viking.gt, a worm well known to anti-malware software vendors at the time, attacked office computers belonging to a large bank in Norway. The worm, most likely residing on an external game site, entered the bank's internal networks via a computer at a branch office and cascaded across roughly 1,000 servers and

© The Author(s) 2016
K.J. Hole, *Anti-fragile ICT Systems*, Simula SpringerBriefs on Computing 1,
DOI 10.1007/978-3-319-30070-2_9

11,000 office PCs in 190 branch offices. This cascade failure occurred because the anti-malware software running on the bank's computers did not stop infections, even though the anti-malware software was updated with an appropriate signature for the worm. During the attack, branch offices could not assist their customers with many tasks and some offices closed.

About 200 individuals worked two shifts to remove the worm. Because the worm disabled the machines' automatic software update mechanism, the worm had to be manually removed from each machine. The vendor's initial upgrade to the anti-malware software was flawed, allowing infected machines to reinfect cleaned machines over internal networks. The bank decided to close all connections to the Internet to protect their internal systems from further external infection. It then took days to remove the malware from the internal networks.

The next section presents a malware spreading model that allows malware to reinfect nodes. This stochastic model is a generalization of the deterministic explanatory model in Chap. 8.

## 9.2 Stochastic Epidemiological Model

Let a networked computer system be infected by different types of malware. The malware's spreading network is modeled as an undirected graph with $M$ edges and $N$ nodes of different types. The node types represent machines with distinct software at the operating system or application layer and the edges represent virtual communication lines. There is at most one edge between two nodes and no edge connects a node to itself. If there is an edge between two nodes, then these nodes are neighbors. The degree $k$ of a node is the number of neighbors. The nodes' average degree is $\langle k \rangle = (2M)/N$.

As noted in Chap. 8, the topology of the spreading network depends on the software layer and the vulnerabilities exploited to spread the malware. We discriminate between an *inhomogeneous* network containing a few nodes, the hubs, with a very large degree $k \gg \langle k \rangle$ and a *homogeneous* network where all nodes have a degree $k \approx \langle k \rangle$. Any spreading network has $L$ different node types $l = 1, 2, \ldots, L$ for $1 \leq L \ll N$. Each node type occurs $N_l$ times. A node chosen uniformly at random is of type $l$ with probability $N_l/N$ for $N = \sum_l N_l$. When $N_l = N/L$, the diversity is equal to the number of node types $L$ with the convention that a monoculture network with only one type has no diversity [50].

A node of arbitrary type $l$ is either susceptible to an infection or it is infected. If an infection is removed from the node, then it immediately becomes susceptible to a new infection. There are $L$ types of malware, where each type of malware infects a particular software platform, that is, node type. Because there are $L$ nodes types with $L$ corresponding malware types, the complete spreading network can be viewed as $L$ disjoint subnet monocultures, each containing a single node type.

Multiple simultaneous malware epidemics are modeled by $L$ susceptible–infected–susceptible (SIS) models [23, 87] operating on the same network topology but affecting $L$ disjoint subnet monocultures. Initially, all the nodes are susceptible. At time step $t = 0$, the model selects uniformly at random $S (\geq 1)$ nodes of each type $l$ and infects them. These $L \cdot S$ initially infected nodes are the seeds. For each time step $t = 1, 2, 3, \ldots$, any infected node of type $l$ infects any susceptible neighbor of type $l$ with *infection probability* $p_l, 0 < p_l \leq 1$. At the same time, any infected node of type $l$ recovers with *recovery probability* $q_l, 0 \leq q_l \leq 1$.

If $q_l > 0$ for some $l$, then a node can repeat the SIS life cycle many times. The result is a stochastic model with long-term dynamics, where it is assumed that the infections and recoveries are updated in a random asynchronous order. When $p_l = 1$ and $q_l = 0$ for all $l$, the SIS models become $L$ susceptible–infected (SI) models. The overall spreading model is deterministic in this case, since malware infects all reachable nodes with 100 % probability. Consequently, the spreading process is completely determined by the network's topology, the configuration of node types, and the selection of seeds. Because no node recovers from an infection, there are no long-term dynamics. The spreading simply stops when all reachable nodes are infected. This special case of $L$ deterministic SI models was first presented in Chap. 8 for $N_l = N/L$.

## 9.3  How to Immunize Unknown Hubs

While we may not know the degrees of many nodes in inhomogeneous spreading networks, it is still possible to immunize hubs in advance of malware outbreaks. The acquaintance immunization strategy [25] provides an elegant solution to the problem of immunizing unknown hubs in a monoculture ($L = 1$): Choose a set of nodes uniformly at random and immunize one arbitrary neighbor per node. While the original set of nodes is unlikely to contain the relatively few hubs in an inhomogeneous network, the randomly selected neighbors are much more likely to be hubs, since many edges are adjacent to high-degree nodes.

We can generalize acquaintance immunization to diverse networks. Assume that it is possible to estimate the number of nodes $N_l$ of each type $l$ in a diverse network, perhaps by estimating the total size of the network and then determining the percentages of different node types in a small part of the network. For some fraction $0 < f < 1$, choose a set of $f \cdot N_l$ nodes of type $l$ uniformly at random such that each node has at least one neighbor of the same type, $l = 1, 2, \ldots, L$. Immunize one randomly selected neighbor of type $l$ per node in the set. When the number of immunized neighbors $f \cdot N_l$ of each type $l$ is large enough, most hubs are immunized [25].

To illustrate acquaintance immunization on diverse spreading networks, we consider an inhomogeneous network with dominant hubs. The network has 10,670 nodes and 22,002 edges. The largest hub has degree 2,312, which is nearly 11 % of the total number of edges. The $L = 7$ node types have different colors and the size of a node is proportional to its degree; that is, hubs are larger than low-degree nodes.

**Fig. 9.1** Acquaintance
immunization of a network
with enlarged hubs at the
*top*. Only immunized nodes
and susceptible hubs are
shown. Note that most hubs
are immunized

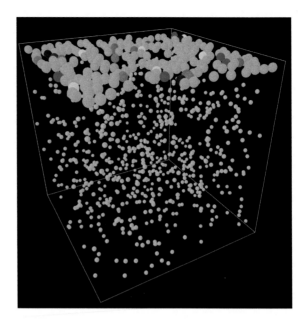

A node turns pink when it is immunized. Let the fraction of immunized neighbors be
$f = 0.04$ (4 %). Figure 9.1 shows only the immunized pink nodes and the remaining
susceptible multicolored hubs after acquaintance immunization. No edges or susceptible low-degree nodes are shown. Note that most of the 216 enlarged hubs are
immunized. Assume $S = 20$ seeds per node type for a total of $7 \cdot 20 = 140$ seeds. Let
$p_l = 0.06$ and $q_l = 0.04$. When acquaintance immunization is performed in advance,
the fraction of infected nodes goes to zero after only a few hundred time steps.

## 9.4   Lower Bound on Required Diversity

In this section we determine a lower bound on the node diversity $L$ needed to make it
very likely that new malware outbreaks will die out before they spread to many nodes.
We assume that all hubs are immunized, even though acquaintance immunization
may miss a few. Because the hubs and their adjacent edges do not partake in the
transmission of malware, we model the spreading network after hub immunization
as a random homogeneous network with $N$ nodes, average degree $z = \langle k \rangle$, and
$N_l = N/L$ nodes of each type, $l = 1, 2, \ldots, L$. The spreading network has a
fixed but arbitrary (thin-tailed) degree distribution. Note that modeling the remaining
spreading network after hub immunization as a random network is an approximation
chosen because random networks are malleable to analysis [23].

The average fraction of infected nodes of type $l$, denoted $h_l$, is estimated by
considering the subset of $N/L$ nodes of type $l$. To estimate $h_l$, we extend an analytical

technique for random networks viewed as homogeneous monocultures ($L = 1$) [23, 87]. Each malware outbreak in a network with $L > 1$ node types operates on a subgraph with $N/L$ nodes of the same type. On average, a node has $z/L$ neighbors in the subgraph because the probability that a node is of type $l$ is $N_l/N = 1/L$. Let the spreading rate be $\rho_l = (p_l z)/(q_l L)$ for $q_l > 0$, $l = 1, 2, \ldots, L$, and view $h_l = h_l(t)$ as a continuous-time variable. Representing the expected change in the fraction of infected nodes as the differential equation

$$\frac{dh_l}{dt} = p_l \frac{z}{L} h_l (1 - h_l) - q_l h_l$$

and imposing the stationary condition $dh_l/dt = 0$, we find that the average fraction of infected nodes saturates at $h_l = 1 - 1/\rho_l$ for $\rho_l > 1$. The fraction $h_l$ goes to zero in finite time when $\rho_l < 1$. For a fixed infection probability $p_l$, recovery probability $q_l$, and average degree $z$, the spreading rate $\rho_l = (p_l z)/(q_l L) < 1$ when the number of node types $L > (p_l z)/q_l$. Consequently, $h_l$ goes to zero.

Since we need $h_l$ to go to zero for all $l$, the needed node diversity is lower bounded by

$$L > z \cdot \max_l \left\{ \frac{p_l}{q_l} \right\}, \tag{9.1}$$

where $z = \langle k \rangle$ is the average node degree of the remaining spreading network after hub immunization. The largest spreading rate essentially determines the required diversity $L$.

It is possible to estimate the lower bound in inequality (9.1) for real malware types by estimating the infection probabilities $p_l$ and recovery probabilities $q_l$. However, the inequality is first and foremost important because it shows that multiple simultaneous malware outbreaks with the ability to reinfect nodes will die out before they can spread far when the software diversity is large enough, given that hubs are immunized.

## 9.5  Discussion and Summary

A combination of acquaintance immunization and node diversity prevents malware with the ability to reinfect nodes from creating long-lasting epidemics. Through immunization of most of the hubs and a sufficient increase in node diversity, malware outbreaks are likely to die out quickly. Hence, acquaintance immunization and node diversity together provide robustness to malware reinfection.

As first stated in Sect. 8.7, graph coloring algorithms can be used to ensure that no (or very few) pairs of neighboring nodes have the same color or node type. Coloring algorithms exploit the topology of static spreading networks to reduce the number of node types needed to prevent malware propagation, compared to our simple approach of just randomly assigning node types. Why, then, are we using this simple approach in both the previous and current chapters when it does not minimize the number of different colors needed to prevent malware spreading? There are two main reasons.

First, while coloring algorithms need central processing to assign node types, our simple scheme requires no central control. We cannot use algorithms requiring central control to assign node types because of their limited scalability. Our goal is a malware-halting technique that scales to millions of nodes. Second, the topologies of the malware spreading networks are not known and, even if they were, networks will vary over time, making it necessary to constantly rerun the coloring algorithms to reassign node types. Hence, we do not let the perfect be the enemy of the good. Instead of trying to come up with sophisticated solutions to make highly complex networks more or less immune to malware spreading, we fight complexity with simplicity [88]. The next chapter suggests and analyzes a simple scalable technique providing anti-fragility to malware with unknown and changing spreading patterns.

# Chapter 10
# Anti-fragility to Malware Spreading

To achieve anti-fragility to malware spreading, this chapter applies the fail fast principle from Chap. 4 to the robust malware-halting technique developed in the two previous chapters. According to the fail fast principle, it is necessary to learn from failures in complex adaptive systems when the impact of the failures are still small. In the case of infectious malware epidemics, once malware is detected on a node in a networked system, other nodes infected by the same malware should be healed and susceptible nodes should be protected from future infections of this malware.

The two previous chapters showed how software diversity and hub immunization could halt malicious software or malware from spreading. This chapter combines compiler-generated software diversity [24, 56, 89], hub immunization, and imperfect malware detection/removal to achieve anti-fragility to the spreading of various types of malware in networked computing systems. The cloud is used to efficiently combine these techniques. The suggested malware-halting technique scales to huge networks because it does not require any tightly coupled interactions or adaptations between groups of devices. The average fraction of infected nodes is reduced compared to the examples in Chap. 8. The technique is of practical interest because malware is an omnipresent and serious security threat [21, 22]. The ideas in this chapter were first presented in [90].

We again study infectious malware, that is, computer worms with different spreading mechanisms. E-mail malware spreading via address lists and mobile phone malware propagating over short-range wireless links generate patterns of infected devices defined by sparse graphs [85], while malware scanning Internet protocol version 4 (IPv4) addresses at random produce dense graphs. We concentrate on sparse spreading networks in this chapter. Rather than trying to accurately model the spreading of real malware instances, we again analyze worst-case spreading where the first attempt to infect a susceptible device always succeeds.

Non-infectious malware strains, such as trojans, spyware, adware, and ransomware, mistakenly downloaded by computer users are viewed as infectious malware with limited spreading ability. We measure malware spreading in a networked computing system by the fraction of infected devices. A system is *fragile* to malware when small outbreaks of different malware strains spread to a large fraction of the

© The Author(s) 2016
K.J. Hole, *Anti-fragile ICT Systems*, Simula SpringerBriefs on Computing 1,
DOI 10.1007/978-3-319-30070-2_10

devices. If the malware strains only spread to a small fraction of the devices, then the system is *robust*. A system under repeated attacks from malware is *anti-fragile* if it first learns to reduce the fraction of infected devices and then manages to keep the fraction small when the malware's spreading mechanism changes.

To achieve anti-fragility in practice, it is advantageous to build on existing and planned automated software mechanisms. We combine compiler-generated diversity, software downloads from application stores, hub immunization, and imperfect malware detection/removal to achieve anti-fragility to malware spreading. An agent-based model randomly adds software diversity to a software monoculture to create a software polyculture with a much reduced fraction of infected devices. The model demonstrates that periodically removing executable code, including unknown malware, from devices and installing new diverse code drastically increase robustness to malware spreading. If imperfect malware detection is added, the model gains a degree of anti-fragility because it can more quickly remove malware and update vulnerable code to keep the fraction of infected devices very small, even when the malware strains have unknown and time-varying spreading.

## 10.1   System Model

As in the two previous chapters, we study a network of interconnected computing devices and consider the devices at the operating system (OS) and application levels. Application stores in the cloud, such as Google Play and iOS App Store, utilize compilers with "diversity engines" to generate binary images for a huge number of devices, producing many different executable images from a much smaller set of OSs and application source codes [24, 89]. As in earlier chapters, we assume that a program's many binary images can be divided into classes such that all members of the same class have a common exploitable vulnerability, while members of different classes have no common exploitable vulnerabilities.

The number of classes measures the program's diversity, assuming roughly equally large classes. Since compiler-driven diversity promises to provide large diversity [24, 77], we forgo any notion of central control over the assignment of software diversity to computing platforms and make no attempt to minimize the use of diversity. This allows us to study the benefit of software diversity in systems with millions of devices. Cloud-based compilations of source codes allow application stores to support large numbers of download requests each day.

A significant fraction of all malware infections is not discovered by traditional signature-based malware detection because modern malware utilizes time-varying code obfuscation to avoid detection based on fixed byte patterns [21]. Emerging cloud-based anti-malware solutions promise to improve automated malware detection [22, 91, 92]. Servers in the cloud deploy heuristic, behavioral, and signature-based techniques to detect different types of malware by processing data collected by clients running on user devices. A cloud solution can also incorporate knowledge from other sources, such as malware honeypots, that is, computers capturing malware.

Despite the protection promised by cloud anti-malware, it is nearly impossible to keep all computing devices in a networked system free from malware at all times. The difficulty of detecting encrypted malicious traffic and the successful use of rootkits to hide malware suggest that automated malware detection will remain imperfect for the foreseeable future [21]. A more realistic goal is to provide a form of "community immunity," where most devices are protected against malware because there is little opportunity for outbreaks to spread. Whereas community immunity usually entails the immunization of nearly all entities in a population, we mainly deploy compiler-generated software diversity to reduce malware spreading. Our goal is not to force the fraction of infected devices to zero but, rather, to keep it very low over time.

We study consecutive outbreaks of different malware types, called *multimalware* outbreaks, because the deployment of multiple malware types is an obvious strategy to counter software diversity. Devices are assumed to automatically remove executable code, including unknown malware, and immediately download new diverse code from application stores on a semi-regular basis. The introduction of imperfect malware detection allows devices to also initiate unscheduled code removal and updates when infections are detected. In severe but rare cases, trained personnel must take a device offline to wipe its entire memory before installing the new software. The following model assumes that the self-repairing and diversity-enhancing approach removes all malware. Because it is hard to remove advanced malware, especially rootkits, from real systems, it is possible to adjust how often the model successful carries out code removals and updates.

### 10.1.1 Model Description

We model multimalware spreading over networked computing devices by a simple graph (no self-loops or parallel edges) with $N$ nodes and a maximum of $L$ node types for $L \ll N$. At time step $t = 0, 1, \ldots$, the graph contains $D = D(t)$ of the $L$ node types, where $D(0) = 1$. The $D$ *active* node types represent classes of binary codes at the OS or application level of the devices' computing platforms; that is, nodes of the same type share an exploitable vulnerability while nodes of different types have no common exploitable vulnerabilities. The edges represent virtual communication lines. The number of active node types $D$ measures the model's time-varying *diversity*.

Two nodes are neighbors if there is an edge between them. A node's degree $k$ is the number of neighbors and $\langle k \rangle$ is the average degree over all nodes. All nodes change type with probability $p$ at each time step to model the automated removal of executable code (including unknown malware), followed by immediate downloads of new diverse code from application stores. One of the $L$ possible node types is selected with probability $1/L$, thus changing the initial monoculture into a polyculture with diversity $L$.

Initially, all nodes are susceptible to malware infections. There is one malware type per node type. All malware types have the same spreading mechanism. Whereas epidemiological models in the literature tend to model a single malware outbreak, we model systems with many outbreaks. One malware outbreak occurs with probability $q$ at each time step. An outbreak initially infects a single susceptible node selected uniformly at random. A newly sick node infects all its susceptible neighbors of the same type during the next time step. Infected nodes change type with probability $r$ at each time step to model the varying degree of imperfect malware detection followed by immediate malware removal and the installation of new diverse code. Any infected node becomes susceptible when it changes type.

It is possible to switch off automated malware detection by setting $r = 0$. We can also set $p = 0$ to disable automated software downloads. A small fraction of nodes can be immunized, that is, made resistant to malware infections. Immunized nodes do not change type or transmit infections to neighbors. As stated in Chap. 8, automated immunization or hardening includes the removal of non-essential software programs, the secure configuration of remaining programs, constant patching, and the use of firewalls and intrusion prevention systems. Other mitigation techniques, such as control-flow integrity [93], that induce code overhead and performance penalties can also be used on selected devices.

## 10.1.2  Model Limitations

As first observed in Chap. 8, it is hard to predict how malware will spread over a networked computing system because the propagation depends on the malware's spreading mechanism, the network topology, changing traffic loads, routing and filtering policies, the choice of communication protocols, and network failures and misconfigurations. Rather than trying to generate accurate spreading patterns under various network conditions, the model displays very fast worst-case malware spreading in which an infectious node immediately infects all its neighbors of the same type.

Although the model cannot predict spreading in a real networked system, it can demonstrate the usefulness of combining software diversity and imperfect malware detection to halt malware spreading. Compared to the model, actual malware is likely to spread slower, because the first attempt to infect a susceptible computing device will not always succeed and not all susceptible devices will be infected because some are unreachable in practice. Hence, it is reasonable to believe that modeled malware halting translates into halting in real systems.

We only study sparse spreading patterns with an average degree $\langle k \rangle$ much lower than the number of nodes $N$. Whereas nodes and edges can be deleted during a model run and new nodes and edges added to simulate changes in the malware's spreading mechanism, nodes cannot change position after they have been created.

## 10.2   Anti-fragility on Static Graphs

A worst-case spreading pattern given by a network with average degree $\langle k \rangle$ is homogeneous when all nodes have degrees $k \approx \langle k \rangle$. To keep the analysis manageable, we first study static spreading patterns represented by homogeneous networks and determine when the system model is anti-fragile to spreading.

Consider a homogeneous network with a single node type at time $t = 0$, $D(0) = 1$. If this monoculture is connected, then it is extremely fragile to malware spreading since a single sick node will infect all nodes as long as no node changes type. The model avoids fragile monocultures by allowing nodes to change type. Each time a node changes type, it selects a particular type with probability $1/L$. Consequently, the number of node types $D(t)$ will grow toward the maximum value $L$. The phase where $D(t)$ changes from one to $L$ will be simulated later. Here, we assume that $D(t) = L$, where $t > t'$ for a small finite time $t'$, and study the model after the fraction of infected nodes starts to fluctuate around a small time-averaged value $f$.

We need to determine an expression for the time-averaged fraction $f$ of infected nodes. Let $Q$ denote the set of susceptible nodes that are infected during $T$ time steps. We first estimate the expected number of infected nodes in $Q$, denoted $E\{|Q|\}$. During each time step, there is a probability $q$ that a single susceptible node is seeded with an infection. The probability that no neighboring node has the same type as this seed is approximately $(1 - 1/L)^{\langle k \rangle}$. If we choose a large diversity $L > \langle k \rangle$ such that this probability is large, then an infection will most likely spread at most from the seed to the nearest neighbors of the same type. Ignoring further spreading, each seed infects, on average, $\langle k \rangle / L < 1$ of its neighbors. Over $T$ time steps, the expected number of seeds is $T \cdot q$ and about $T \cdot q \cdot \langle k \rangle / L$ susceptible neighbors will be infected, since the average fraction $f$ of infected nodes is small. The expected number of susceptible nodes becoming infected during the period $T$ is thus estimated by $E\{|Q|\} \approx T \cdot q \cdot (1 + \langle k \rangle / L)$.

Next, we determine the expected number of infected nodes that become susceptible during $T$ time steps. All $N$ nodes in a network change type with probability $p$ to model periodic downloads of diverse software. Let $P$ denote the set of infected nodes that change type (and become susceptible) due to periodic software downloads. We need to determine the expected size of $P$, denoted $E\{|P|\}$. The expected number of type changes over a period $T$ is $p \cdot N \cdot T$. Since the fraction of infected nodes is $f$, the expected number of infected nodes that change type is $E\{|P|\} = f \cdot p \cdot N \cdot T$.

The remaining infected nodes at a time step detect their infections with probability $r$. Let $R$ be the set of infected nodes that change type (and become susceptible) due to malware detection followed by an immediate software download. We also need to determine the expected size $E\{|R|\}$. The expected number of infected nodes is $f \cdot N \cdot T$ and the expected number of infected nodes changing type is $E\{|R|\} = r \cdot f \cdot N \cdot T$.

Over $T$ time steps, the two sets $P$ and $R$ overlap. The total number of unique nodes changing type and becoming susceptible is given by the union $P \cup R$. The expected size is of this union is $E\{|P \cup R|\} = E\{|P|\} + E\{|R|\} - E\{|P \cap R|\} = pfNT + rfNT - prfNT = fNT(p + r - pr)$. The expected number of nodes

changing type and becoming susceptible must be equal to the expected number of
new infected nodes to maintain a stable time-averaged fraction $f$ of infected nodes.
Hence, the relation $E\{|P \cup R|\} = E\{|Q|\}$ results in the approximation

$$f \approx \frac{q\,[1 + \langle k \rangle / L]}{(p + r - pr)N} \qquad (10.1)$$

for homogeneous networks with diversity $L > \langle k \rangle$.

Equation (10.1) shows that it is possible to maintain a small fraction $f$ of infected
nodes, even if malware detection is switched off ($r = 0$), by adjusting the software
download probability $p$. Note that this property is based on the assumption that
malware is removed during the software update process. Let $p$ and $r$ be small such
that the value of $pr$ is negligible compared to $p + r$. When malware detection is
switched on ($r > 0$), the fraction of infected nodes reduces further for a fixed
probability $p$. Hence, anti-fragile systems using imperfect detection and removal
of new malware further reduce the fraction of infected devices, compared to robust
systems that merely remove old code and download new diverse code periodically.


## 10.2.1   Simulations of Anti-fragility on Static Networks

To validate Eq. (10.1), we consider smartphones and other handheld computing
devices that communicate via short-range Wi-Fi and Bluetooth links [85]. Infectious
malware types can copy themselves to new devices by opening wireless connections. Malware can also propagate directly between Wi-Fi access points via wireless
connections [94]. We represent the worst-case spreading patterns by homogeneous
proximity networks. The system model was programmed in NetLogo [46] and generates a proximity network with average node degree $\langle k \rangle$ by first placing $N$ nodes
uniformly at random on a square. An edge is then added between a randomly chosen node and its closest neighbor in Euclidean distance. More edges are similarly
added until the network has the desired average degree. Self-loops and multiple edges
between nodes are not allowed.

Simulations were run on networks with $N = 5{,}000$ nodes, $L = 20$ node types, and
different average degrees $\langle k \rangle$. The outbreak probability was $q = 10^{-2}$, the software
download probability $p = 10^{-5}$, and the malware detection probability $r = 10^{-3}$.
Table 10.1 lists the observed average, minimum, and maximum fraction of infected
nodes over 100 runs, where each value was averaged over the last 10,000 time steps
of a run. The table also reports an estimate of the average fraction obtained from
Eq. (10.1). The good agreement between the simulated and calculated values shows
that the expression can provide good estimates of the average fraction of infected
nodes. Other model runs with different parameter values confirm the agreement
between simulated and calculated values.

**Table 10.1** The estimated average fractions of infected nodes in proximity networks with 5,000 nodes and increasing average node degree

| Proximity networks | | | | |
|---|---|---|---|---|
| Average degree | 5 | 6 | 7 | 8 |
| Estimated frac. | 0.25 % | 0.26 % | 0.27 % | 0.28 % |
| Simulated frac. | 0.26 % | 0.27 % | 0.28 % | 0.30 % |
| (max., min.) | (+0.09, −0.08) | (+0.08, −0.1) | (+0.11, −0.07) | (+0.16, −0.11) |

The corresponding simulated fractions are averaged over 100 runs, with the largest observed deviations shown in parentheses

### 10.2.2 Anti-fragility on Large Static Networks

Since there is agreement between the average fractions of infected nodes obtained from the simulations and from Eq. (10.1), we use the equation to study anti-fragility to malware spreading on very large homogeneous networks. The required frequency of software download $p$ and the frequency of malware detection $r$ decrease as the size of a network grows, because $p + r$ is proportional to $1/N$. Hence, anti-fragility to malware occurs on large model networks for practical download and detection frequencies.

Consider a homogeneous network with 100 million nodes, that is, $N = 10^8$, and average degree $\langle k \rangle \ll L$. For outbreak frequency $q = 10^{-2}$ and an average fraction of infected nodes $f = 10^{-3}$, we have from Eq. (10.1) that $p + r \approx q/(fN) = 10^{-7}$. If each time step in the model is one second long, then there is a new malware outbreak every 100 seconds, on average. The fraction of infected nodes is maintained when the download frequency is $p \approx 10^{-7}$ without malware detection ($r = 0$), that is, each device has to download and install new software after about 116 days. If malware detection is added to our example, then the average fraction of infected devices is reduced. For $r = 10^{-4}$ and $p = 10^{-7}$, we have $f \approx 10^{-6}$. The calculations illustrate that anti-fragility to malware spreading scales to very large homogeneous networks.

## 10.3 Anti-fragility on Time-Varying Graphs

We now consider a modified system model with an unknown and time-varying worst-case spreading pattern that remains sparse over time. Even if the spreading mechanism varies, the spreading is mostly limited to the neighbors of the nodes seeded with infections as long as the spreading pattern remains homogeneous and the diversity remains much larger than the changing average degree.

We therefore study inhomogeneous spreading patterns containing a small fraction of nodes, called *hubs*, with degree $k_h$ much larger than the time-varying average degree. A hub and its $k_h$ neighbors form a star graph with the hub at the center. If all $k_h + 1$ nodes have a uniform distribution of $L$ node types, then there are roughly

$k_h/L$ neighbors of the same type as the hub. A susceptible hub is infected each time one of the neighbors of the same type is infected. A reinfected hub again infects all susceptible neighbors of the same type, ensuring a total of $k_h/L$ infected neighbors.

Since a hub's $k_h$ neighbors constitute a significant fraction of all nodes in a worst-case spreading pattern, we may very well have $k_h \gg L$. This is why hubs are referred to as super-spreaders, even in software polycultures. Note that malware does not need to be infectious for a hub to be a super-spreader; for example, a hub can be a popular website infected by malware that is inadvertently downloaded by many users accessing the site. While the non-infectious malware does not spread any further after the downloads, the number of infected devices $k_h/L$ is still large.

Similarly, if the hubs' neighbors tend to have small degrees, most of the spreading of infectious malware will also be confined to the hubs' neighbors. Even when a hub regularly changes type, there will still be roughly $k_h/L$ neighbors of the same type as long as all nodes have a uniform distribution of types. Over time, a hub that changes type will reinfect many neighbors as long as at least a few neighbors of different types are infected.

If hubs are connected in a small subnetwork and several hubs have the same type, then a large fraction of all nodes in a worst-case spreading network is infected very quickly. Hence, we need to "neutralize" hubs, especially tightly connected hubs, to make the actual spreading pattern more homogeneous such that, for any susceptible node of degree $k$, the expected number of neighbors of the same type is negligible ($k/L \ll 1$).

The following three malware simulations with different spreading patterns show that hubs can be immunized to gain anti-fragility to multimalware spreading. Rather than presenting plots averaged over many runs to obtain smooth curves, the figures plot single runs to better demonstrate how anti-fragile systems would actually behave.

### 10.3.1   Simulations of Anti-fragility

In the first simulation, the NetLogo model generates a time-varying spreading pattern. A model run starts with a proximity network with 2,000 nodes, average degree $\langle k \rangle = 4$, maximum degree 10, and diversity $D(0) = 1$. Initially, malware detection is turned off ($r = 0$). The fraction of infected nodes plotted in Fig. 10.1 reduces from about 91 to 8 % as the model changes from a fragile monoculture to a more robust polyculture with diversity $L = 5$. When malware detection is turned on ($r = 10^{-2}$), the fraction reduces further to 0.1 %. The plot confirms the advantage of introducing software diversity and applying imperfect malware detection.

Next, 75 % of the nodes and their adjacent edges are deleted and the network is regrown using the preferential attachment technique [95], with each new node connected to three existing nodes. The new nodes have a uniform distribution of node types. This simulated change in spreading mechanism causes the original homogeneous spreading pattern to change into an inhomogeneous spreading pattern. The new spreading pattern has an average degree $\langle k \rangle = 4.8$ and a maximum degree 33.

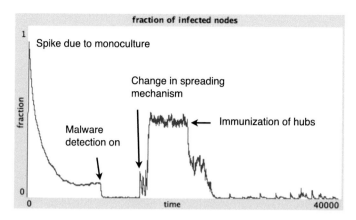

**Fig. 10.1** The fraction of infected nodes in a changing network with 2,000 nodes, outbreak probability $q = 10^{-2}$, download probability $p = 10^{-3}$, and diversity $L = 5$. The plot illustrates the effects of increasing diversity, malware detection, a change in spreading mechanism, and hub immunization

The fraction of infected nodes increases to roughly 45 % because the diversity $L$ is not large enough to prevent spreading from the new hubs, even though malware detection is still on. The sharp increase in the fraction of infected nodes illustrates that the malware halting is fragile to changes in the spreading pattern when the diversity is too small.

Finally, the 61 nodes with the largest degrees are immunized. When these hubs and their adjacent edges are ignored because they no longer contribute to malware spreading, the remaining spreading pattern has average degree $\langle k \rangle = 3.8$ and maximum degree 14. The fraction of infected nodes reduces to roughly 0.6 %, demonstrating the need to immunize super-spreaders in real networks to obtain more homogeneous spreading patterns.

In the second simulation, the NetLogo model starts with an inhomogeneous email network with 1,133 nodes, average degree $\langle k \rangle = 9.6$, maximum degree 71, and diversity $L = 8$. The largest hubs are immunized before the model run starts. As shown in Fig. 10.2, the fraction of infected nodes reduces to roughly 1 % as the monoculture turns into a polyculture. The model then erases 75 % of all nodes as before and creates an inhomogeneous network with 2,000 nodes. No new nodes are immunized and their types are uniformly distributed. The new subgraph of susceptible nodes has average degree $\langle k \rangle = 4.7$ and maximum degree 44. Unlike in the first simulation, there is no large change in the fraction of infected nodes in Fig. 10.2 because the diversity, the remaining immunized nodes, and the malware detection probability ($r = 10^{-2}$) together prevent significant spreading. The plot shows that the malware halting can be made robust to changes in the spreading pattern.

In the third simulation, the NetLogo model utilizes a static inhomogeneous spreading pattern with 10,670 nodes, 36 hubs that form a small connected subgraph, and many nodes with a low degree $k \approx \langle k \rangle = 4.1$. The hubs' degrees range from

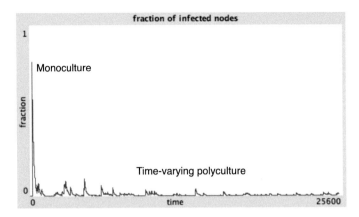

**Fig. 10.2** The fraction of infected nodes in a time-varying e-mail network with outbreak probability $q = 10^{-2}$, download probability $p = 10^{-3}$, malware detection probability $r = 10^{-2}$, and diversity $L = 8$. Note that there is no visible change in the fraction when the spreading network changes

2,312 down to 102. In a real network, any immunization of hubs is likely to be imperfect because some infected hubs are not detected or because some hardened hubs still become infected. The model utilizes acquaintance immunization to simulate imperfect cloud-based detection and immunization of infected hubs [25]. This immunization technique chooses a set of nodes uniformly at random and immunizes one arbitrary neighbor per node. While the original set of nodes is unlikely to contain the few hubs in the network, the randomly selected neighbors are much more likely to be hubs, since many edges are adjacent to high-degree nodes.

Figure 10.3 plots the fraction of infected nodes. The fraction decreases as the diversity grows to $L = 14$ but stabilizes around 11 % because the hubs are not immunized. When acquaintance immunization selects 2 % of the nodes, all but three

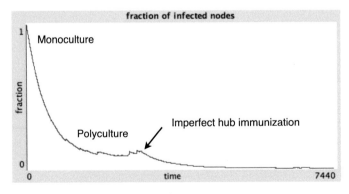

**Fig. 10.3** The fraction of infected nodes in a static network with 10,670 nodes, outbreak probability $q = 10^{-1}$, download probability $p = 10^{-3}$, malware detection probability $r = 10^{-3}$, and diversity $L = 14$

of the hubs are immunized. The fraction of infected nodes reduces to about 0.1 %. Figure 10.3 illustrates that imperfect detection and immunization of hubs reduce the fraction of infected nodes, even when the spreading pattern contains a subnetwork of tightly connected hubs.

Additional simulations with varying parameter values confirm the model behavior reported. In particular, simulations using acquaintance immunization confirm the adequacy of imperfect hub immunization. The additional simulations further strengthen the claim that compiler-generated software diversity, periodic downloads of software from application stores, and imperfect malware detection/removal together provide a networked computing system with a degree of anti-fragility to multimalware spreading.

## 10.4 Discussion

The anti-fragile malware-halting technique scales to large networked systems because compiler-generated software diversity and malware detection can be implemented as cloud services. While empirical work is needed to determine the real-world performance of the combined services, it is encouraging that there exist commercial anti-malware solutions running in the cloud. According to Franz's research group [24, 89], it is cost-effective to compile diverse software in the cloud. Furthermore, the impact of software diversity on the runtime performance is small and it is possible to securely patch diverse software. Still, challenges remain.

While acquaintance immunization is useful for simulating imperfect detection and immunization of hubs, the strategy is not the best choice for real networked systems, because many potential super-spreaders, such as popular websites, are known. The challenge is to ensure that the owners of potential super-spreaders harden their systems. Users could be warned to stay away from infected websites, making it necessary for owners to remove the malware and harden the systems to get their users back. At the time of this writing, Google informs users and webmasters of unsafe websites (http://google.com/transparencyreport/safebrowsing).

Netflix's decision to induce failures in their production system to repeatedly increase robustness to downtime raises the question of whether to use infectious "goodware" to improve the detection of susceptible devices and speed up the learning process leading to anti-fragility to malware spreading. While ethical questions are associated with this approach, it is worth investigating.

Although users today regularly download software from application stores, more work is needed to create self-repairing (up to a point) devices that remove malware and install diverse software in a way acceptable to users.

**What to learn from Part III**

Part III analyzed how to prevent infectious malware from spreading over huge networks of computing devices. Through a series of analyses, we developed a malware-halting technique that stops frequent multimalware outbreaks with an unknown and time-varying spreading mechanism. The technique combines application stores with compiler-generated software diversity, imperfect malware detection, and the semi-periodic reinstallation of software on devices. If compiler-generated software diversity and malware detection are realized in the cloud, then the malware-halting technique scales to huge networks, because it does not require any tightly coupled interactions or adaptations between groups of computing devices.

More efficient malware-halting techniques exist that require less software diversity to halt malware outbreaks on spreading networks with known and unchanging topologies. The problem with these techniques is that the topologies of spreading networks are rarely known in practice. Furthermore, the topologies change over time as the malware writers change the spreading mechanisms. Finally, the previously known techniques require a high degree of central control, limiting the ability to scale to millions of devices. To ensure scaling, we relinquished central control and made a strategical decision to not let the perfect be the enemy of the good. Hence, instead of trying to minimize the needed software diversity, we focused on creating a simple technique that takes advantage of existing and proposed technologies to halt frequent multimalware outbreaks with unknown and changing spreading mechanisms.

# Part IV
# Anomaly Detection

# Chapter 11
# The HTM Learning Algorithm

According to the fail fast principle in Chap. 4, we need to learn from systems' abnormal behavior and downright failures to achieve anti-fragility to classes of negative events. The earlier we can detect problems, the smaller the negative consequences are and the faster we can start learning how to improve the systems. Since humans are not good at detecting anomalies, especially in streaming data from large cloud applications, a form of automatic anomaly detection is needed. There are many ways to detect anomalies, depending on which complex adaptive system we consider. For example, Internet banking solutions employ a rich set of heuristics to detect fraud [26]. This first chapter of Part IV introduces a general learning algorithm based on Hawkins's developing theory of how the brain learns, called hierarchical temporal memory (HTM) [27, 96]. The HTM learning algorithm, or just HTM, is used in the next chapter to detect anomalies in a system's behavior. HTM was earlier referred to as the cortical learning algorithm.

The underlying basis for the HTM learning algorithm is not easy to understand and the algorithm itself is still being developed. To grasp HTM's novelty and importance, the current chapter first discusses the approach to learning taken by traditional artificial intelligence (AI) research, as well as efforts to "train" artificial neural networks to realize particular input–output mappings defined by data "training sets." Second, the chapter outlines why HTM is an improvement over these earlier approaches. Finally, it provides a fairly detailed description of the HTM learning algorithm (with some algorithmic details left out to ease understanding).

While Hawkins' general theory on how the brain works is very interesting, this chapter only provides enough information to understand the major steps of the HTM learning algorithm. The reader wanting to know more about the theory behind HTM should study Hawkins' book *On Intelligence* written with Sandra Blakeslee [27]. More technical information on HTM is given in a white paper [96] by Numenta (http://numenta.com), which was set up to develop the algorithm for both commercial and scientific use. An open source project, called the Numenta platform for intelligent computing (NuPIC) (http://numenta.org), provides HTM program code and documentation. YouTube (see also http://numenta.com/learn) has a growing number

© The Author(s) 2016
K.J. Hole, *Anti-fragile ICT Systems*, Simula SpringerBriefs on Computing 1,
DOI 10.1007/978-3-319-30070-2_11

of talks by Hawkins and others at Numenta on different aspects of HTM. Ryan Price [97] and Michael Galetzka [98] have studied the capabilities and performance of HTM. This chapter is mainly based on information provided by the above sources.

## 11.1  The Problem with Classical AI Research

Learning to recognize known patterns and predict future patterns remains a major challenge for AI, because any autonomous agent needs these abilities to operate successfully in a changing environment. Decades of classical AI research, as well as all the work carried in the 1980s and early 1990s to train artificial neural networks, have not been able to replicate human learning [99, 100, 101]. The main mistake, according to Hawkins [27], was not understanding how the human brain learns and, instead, treating the brain as a computer that could be programmed to produce intelligent behavior. The goal of classical AI was to develop algorithms that would first match and then later surpass human intelligence. Unfortunately, the programs developed were only good at the particular task for which they were designed. The programs did not have the ability to generalize or to show flexibility in the face of changing circumstances. Finally, there were significant unsolved problems on how to represent knowledge in computers.

The author of this book was among the many postdoctoral researchers in the early 1990s developing algorithms to train simple models of neural networks. After much work by many scientists, it became evident that, while these trainable neural network models could learn relatively small problem instances, they did not scale to handle large instances due to an exponential increase in training time and a limited ability to generalize to new circumstances. More recent deep learning algorithms for multilayer neural networks solve larger problem instances and have many interesting applications [102]. However, as for the earlier learning algorithms, deep learning still requires custom training in batch mode for specific tasks and does not continuously learn like the brain.

The limited success of classical AI and neural network research has made many scientists suspect that the brain does not run a large collection of specialized learning algorithms. Other scientists still believe that specialized learning algorithms are needed to achieve a high degree of intelligence. Only future research will show who is correct.

## 11.2  An Alternative Approach to Learning

Hawkins [27] believes the best way to understand how the brain learns is to use its biology as guidance while thinking about learning as an algorithmic problem with a solution implementable on computers, perhaps in the cloud, or, even better, in silicon. Not everybody agrees that the brain is an algorithmic machine (or Turing machine)

[103]. Some scientists and philosophers believe the brain to be a different type of machine based on quantum effects [104, 105, 106]. Here, we do not discuss whether the brain is a quantum computer, since HTM learning is purely algorithmic.

Hawkins has based HTM on a 1978 hypothesis by Vernon Mountcastle [107]. It states that the neocortex uses essentially the same learning algorithm to process the signals from all of the body's sensory organs. HTM is a general learning algorithm and a memory system storing invariant representations of physical structures and abstract concepts. While a traditional specialized AI learning algorithm must be programmed in great detail, HTM is self-learning. Furthermore, whereas artificial neural networks must be trained offline using particular training sets, HTM learns in real time as the data come in. Finally, unlike artificial neural networks, which require retraining when the world changes, HTM is able to forget old representations and learn new representations in real time.

HTM is based on the assumption that the world has structure and is therefore predictable. The world is not chaotic and not homogeneous but complex. The complex but structured behavior of the world allows HTM to learn by creating invariant representations of common patterns reported by the senses. The patterns occur in sequences, enabling HTM to predict future behavior based on earlier experienced behavior. Here, a sequence is a set of patterns that generally accompany each other but not always in a fixed order. The important point is that patterns of a sequence follow each other in time, although the order may vary. HTM is adaptable, allowing it to learn changes in the environment. Old memories are removed and new memories are formed. While HTM models the processing of sensory streams for human vision, touch, hearing, and language, it can also be exposed to non-human sensory input streams such as web traffic, data from cloud computing infrastructures, financial market data, and weather data [96].

## 11.3 The Brain's Neocortex

To understand how the HTM learning algorithm works, it is advantageous to first study its biological basis [27, 96]. HTM is modeled after the structure and operation of the neocortex, or just *cortex*, in the brain. The cortex is responsible for learning. It is a sheet of neural tissue approximately $1,000\,cm^2$ in area and 2.5 mm thick. The cortex looks like a dinner napkin wrapped around the older areas of the brain. The cortex contains at least 30 billion nerve cells, or *neurons*. It consists of six layers formed by variations in the density of cell bodies, cell types, and cell connections. There are five layers of cells and one non-cellular layer. During early development, the cortex divides itself into dozens of functional areas, or regions, based on experience and needs. The function of a region is determined by the information that flows into it. Note that a region comprises all six layers of the cortex. In the following, we consider three important aspects of the neocortex and its neurons.

### 11.3.1  Communication

Classical artificial neural networks model the function of a neuron as a weighted summation of inputs followed by a non-linear operation on the sum. We now know from neuroscience that cortical neurons carry out much more complex operations. An important reason why HTM improves on previous attempts to train neural networks is that HTM utilizes a radically different neuron model, heavily inspired by cortical neurons. The neurons in the cortex communicate with each other via electrical and chemical signals. The signals are the basis of memory and learning in the cortex. As depicted in Fig. 11.1, a typical neuron consists of the cell body, or soma, many dendrites, and a single axon. The branch-like dendrites receive incoming signals from other neurons and the axon and its terminal branches transmit outgoing signals to other neurons. Some axons are coated with myelin, a fatty substance that insulates the axon and increases the speed of communication. Signals pass between neurons at connections called synapses. Note from Fig. 11.1 that neurons do not touch. There is a microscopic gap, denoted the synaptic cleft (see inset), between the axon of one neuron and the dendrite of another.

The signaling occurs roughly as follows: When neuron *A* receives a chemical signal from another neuron, neuron *A* becomes electrically charged relative to the surrounding fluid outside its membrane. The electrical charge travels down the axon, away from *A*'s soma, until it reaches a synapse. Inside the synapse is a group of storage sites, denoted vesicles, containing chemicals manufactured by the soma. When the electrical charge arrives at the synapse, it causes these vesicles to fuse with the synapse's cell membrane, spilling molecules, called neurotransmitters, into the

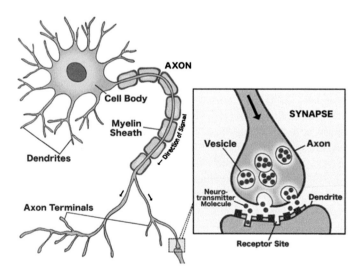

**Fig. 11.1** Signal propagating down an axon to the dendrites of the next cells (figure from http://urbanchildinstitute.org/why-0-3/baby-and-brain)

synaptic cleft. The neurotransmitters move across the synaptic cleft to one of neuron *B*'s dendrites, where they bind with receptor sites in the dendrite's membrane. Neuron *B* develops an electrical charge, the charge travels down its axon, and the described process repeats itself.

While some cortical regions receive input directly from the body's sensory organs, other regions receive input only after it has passed through intermediate regions. The regions are connected via large bundles of axons or fibers. Information flows in parallel over these fibers at all times. The regions process a continuous stream of signals that create patterns in space and time inside the neocortex. The cortex does not experience the world directly; it only has access to patterns coming from the sensory organs. These patterns all have the same format inside the brain, allowing the cortex's different regions to use the same learning algorithm.

### 11.3.2  Memory

The cortex is not some kind of parallel computer that makes many computations on input patterns to create output patterns. Instead, the cortex rapidly retrieves outputs from its huge memory. All memories in the cortex are stored in the synaptic connections between neurons. While both the cortex and computers have memories, there are large differences: The cortex stores sequences of patterns, it recalls patterns auto-associatively, and it stores invariant patterns in hierarchies.

In more detail, the memory of the cortex automatically stores sequences of patterns. Memory recall almost always follows a path of association. Auto-associativity simply means that patterns are associated with themselves. An auto-associative memory can retrieve a complete pattern from a partial or noisy input sequence. This is true for both spatial and temporal patterns. The cortex is constantly completing patterns from noisy and partial inputs.

Regions are connected in hierarchies. Regions at a low level of a hierarchy store simple physical and abstract objects. These objects are combined into larger objects in higher regions. Simple objects can be a part of many hierarchies. Each region forms invariant representations of objects. The invariant representations allow the cortex to recognize faces and physical objects, although the light, viewing angle, and surroundings change all the time. The higher layers of the cortex combine information from the lower layers to understand multi-sensory inputs over time, for example, a film with both sound and moving images.

### 11.3.3  Predictions

The cortex combines the invariant representations with new inputs to make predictions about everything a human sees, feels, and hears. According to Hawkins [27], prediction is the primary function of the cortex and the basis for intelligence. We are interested in the cortex's ability to predict, because an anomaly is detected when a prediction is violated. The reader should know that a great deal of information also flows downward in the hierarchies of the cortex. While these feedback connections are crucial to understanding how the brain creates behavior, they do not play an important role in the current version of HTM and will not be discussed here.

## 11.4   Overview of HTM

The HTM learning algorithm models how learning occurs in a single layer of the cortex. Input to the algorithm is a continuous stream of input patterns from some kind of system. HTM builds sparse, invariant representations of pattern sequences representing repeated structures in the input stream. The algorithm learns which patterns are likely to follow each other, thus learning to predict future patterns. When the HTM receives a novel pattern, it will try to match it to stored patterns. Because inputs never repeat in exactly the same way, invariance of the stored sequences is vital to the ability to recognize inputs.

Time plays a crucial role in HTM. Predictions can only be made on the basis of a sequence of earlier received patterns. Sometimes it is enough to know the previous pattern most recently received while at other times it is also necessary to know patterns received earlier. The ability to predict using variable-length sequences of patterns is due to the variable order memory of HTM. Note that HTM does not understand the meaning of patterns; it only knows what patterns are likely to follow particular observed patterns.

### 11.4.1   Sparse Distributed Representation

HTM generates internal sparse distributed representations (SDRs) of the input patterns. An SDR is given by a binary vector with a fixed number of bits. Different vector lengths are possible. A vector can contain 2,048 bits, only 2% of which are ones, called active bits. The zero bits are the inactive bits. The individual bits in an SDR have semantic meaning, unlike, for example, the dense eight-bit ASCII code, where all bit patterns are used and the characters are assigned bit patterns randomly.

In an SDR, two inputs with similar semantic meaning must have similar binary vector representations, that is, they must have many equal bits when the vectors are compared position by position. This happens naturally for visually similar black and white pictures, while the binary representations of natural numbers with nearly the same values may not have a single bit in common, for example, $7 = 0111_2$ and $8 = 1000_2$. The SDR property is vital to HTM's ability to learn [27]. It is therefore often necessary to recode input data to HTM to ensure that vectors sharing active bits have similar semantic meaning. If the encoded input vectors are dense, then HTM creates a sparse representation.

Ahmad and Hawkins [108] have developed exact bounds on HTM's level of fault tolerance and robustness to noise. The bounds show that the use of SDRs makes it easy to construct HTM systems that are very robust to perturbations.

## 11.4.2 Proximal Dendrite Segments

HTM arranges artificial cells in 2,048 columns, with 32 cells in each column. Conceptually, the columns are arranged in a two-dimensional array, as illustrated in Fig. 11.2. Note that only a small part of the array is shown. Figure 11.3 illustrates how all the cells in a column share a single proximal dendrite segment receiving feed-forward input. Each column has potential connections to a random selection of the bits in an input vector to HTM. These bits are called the potential bits or the potential pool. The status of the connections is determined by the synapses in Fig. 11.3.

HTM uses the concept of *permanence* to change the connectedness of synapses. Permanence is a scalar value ranging from zero to one. It is assigned to a synapse to represent the degree of connectedness between the axon and the dendrite. A permanence value of zero represents a potential synapse that is not valid and has not progressed toward becoming a valid synapse. A permanence value above a threshold (typically 0.2) represents a synapse that has just connected but could easily be unconnected. A high permanence value, for example, 0.9, represents a synapse that is connected and cannot easily be unconnected. When a synapse's permanence is above a threshold, it is connected with weight one. Below the threshold, it is unconnected with weight zero. Note that there is no individual weighting of synaptic connections as in classical neural networks. Instead, HTM has the ability to create and remove these connections. According to Hawkins [27], HTM achieves a higher information

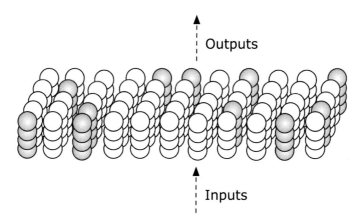

**Fig. 11.2** HTM contains columns of cells with active cells shown in *gray*. When there is no prior state, all or none of the cells in a column are active

**Fig. 11.3** The cells in a
column share a proximal
dendrite, with synapses
represented by *small black
circles*. A *solid circle*
represents a valid synapse
connection with a
permanence value above the
connection threshold and an
*empty circle* represents a
potential synapse connection
with a permanence value
below the connection
threshold. Feed-forward
input activates a column after
a local inhibition step if
enough valid synapses are
connected to active input bits

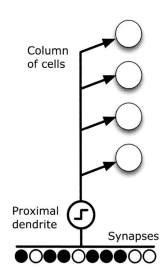

storage capacity by forming and removing synaptic connections than changing the
weights of permanent connections.

Each column determines its activation from the input vector by summing the
input bits in positions with permanence larger than the threshold. The sum of the
bits in these positions constitutes the *overlap score*. The higher the score, that is,
the more active ones, the more overlap between the input and the pattern represented
by the column. Columns with the greatest overlap (strongest activations) inhibit,
or deactivate, columns with weaker activations. The inhibition function achieves a
relatively constant percentage of (about 2 %, or 40) active columns, even when the
number of input bits that are active varies significantly. The result is an SDR of the
input encoded by which columns are active and inactive after inhibition.

### 11.4.3  Distal Dendrite Segments

In addition to the single proximal dendrite segment, a cell has about 130 distal
dendrite segments, each with roughly 40 synapses. The distal segments receive lateral
input from nearby cells. Figure 11.4 shows the distal dendrites and illustrates the
cell's states. The set of potential synapses connects to a subset of other cells within a
neighborhood defined by a "learning radius." A dendrite segment forms connections
to cells that were active together at an earlier time, thus remembering the activation
state of other cells in the neighborhood. If the same cellular activation pattern is
encountered again by one of its segments, that is, the number of active synapses on
any segment is above a threshold, the cell will enter a predictive state indicating that
feed-forward input is expected to result in column activation soon.

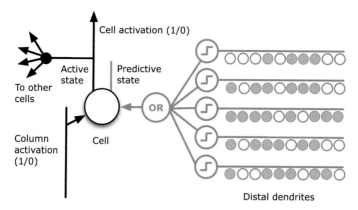

**Fig. 11.4** Each distal dendrite segment of a cell has synapse connections to other cells within the neighborhood. A *solid gray circle* represents a valid synapse connection to another cell and an *empty circle* represents a potential synapse connection. The cell enters a predictive state if at least one of its dendrite segments is connected to enough active cells. A cell's binary-valued predictive state is not propagated. Column activation due to feed-forward input via the proximal dendrite is shown in *black* in the *bottom left*. The binary-valued active state is the feed-forward output of the cell and is also propagated to other cells via lateral connections depicted in the *upper left*

A cell is active due to feed-forward input via the proximal dendrite or lateral connections via the distal dendrite segments. The former is called the *active state* and the latter is called the *predictive state* (see Fig. 11.4). Only the feed-forward active state is connected to other cells in the region. The predictive state is internal to the cell and is not propagated. The complete output of HTM is a binary vector representing the active states of all cells.

## 11.5 The Three Steps of HTM

At each discrete time instance, HTM carries out three steps on the new input. The following descriptions of the steps, detailed in the next sections, are taken from [96]:

**Step 1**    Create an SDR of the input by activating whole columns.
**Step 2**    Place the input in context by selecting among cells in active columns.
**Step 3**    Predict future patterns from learned transitions between SDRs.

### 11.5.1 Make an SDR of the Input

The first step determines the active columns of cells in HTM (see Fig. 11.2). Each column is connected to a subset of the input bits via the synapses on a proximal dendrite. Subsets for different columns may overlap but they are not equal. Consequently, different input patterns result in different levels of activation of the columns. The columns with the strongest activation inhibit columns with weaker activation. The size of the inhibition area around a column is adjustable and can span from very small to the entire region. The inhibition mechanism ensures a sparse representation of the input. If only a few input bits change, some columns will receive a few more or a few less active one inputs, but the set of active columns is not likely to change much. Therefore, similar input patterns will map to a relatively stable set of active columns.

HTM learns by forming and unforming connections between cells. Learning occurs by updating the permanence values of the synapses. Only the active columns increment the permanence value of synapses connected to active bits and decrement otherwise. Columns that do not become active for a long period do not learning anything. To not waste columns, the overlap scores of these columns are "boosted" to ensure that all columns partake in the learning of patterns.

## 11.5.2   Represent the Input in Context of Previous Inputs

Cells can be in one of three states. If a cell is active due to feed-forward input, then it is in the active state. If the cell is active due to lateral connections to other nearby cells, however, then it is in the predictive state; otherwise it is in the inactive state.

The second step converts the columnar representation of the input into a new representation that includes the past context. The new representation is formed by activating a subset of the cells within each column, typically only one cell per column. The rule used to activate cells is as follows: When a column becomes active, HTM checks all the cells in the column. If one or more cells in the column are already in the predictive state, only those cells become active. If no cells in the column are in the predictive state, then all the cells become active. The rule can be understood as follows: If an input pattern is expected, then HTM confirms that expectation by activating only the cells in the predictive state. If the input pattern is unexpected, then HTM activates all the cells in the column to signal that the input occurred unexpectedly.

By selecting different active cells in each active column, HTM can represent the exact same input differently in different contexts. Figure 11.5 illustrates how HTM can represent the sequence AB as part of two larger sequences CABF and HABG. The same columns have active cells in both cases but the active cells differ. If there is no prior state and therefore no context or prediction, all the cells in a column will become active when the column becomes active. This scenario occurs especially when HTM first starts processing input (see Fig. 11.2).

**Fig. 11.5** The sequence AB is part of two larger sequences. The same active columns represent AB in both cases but the active cells differ because the larger sequences are different

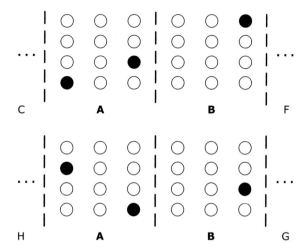

## 11.5.3  Make Prediction from Current and Previous Inputs

The third and final step makes a prediction of likely new input. The prediction is based on the representation formed in the second step, which includes context from all previous input patterns. When HTM makes a prediction, all cells that are likely to become active due to future feed-forward input are changed to the predictive state. Because the representations are sparse, multiple predictions can be made at the same time instance. Together the cells in the predictive state represent HTM's prediction(s) for the next input.

The predictive state of any cell in HTM is determined by its distal segments. A segment connects to cells via synapses on distal dendrites. If enough of these cells are active, then the segment becomes active (see Fig. 11.4). A cell switches to the predictive state when it has at least one active segment. However, a cell that is already active from the second step does not switch to the predictive state. Learning occurs by adjusting the permanence values of the synapses on active segments at every time step. The permanence of a synapse is only updated when a predicted cell actually becomes active during the next time instance. The permanence of a synapse connecting to an active cell is increased while the permanence of a synapse to an inactive cell is decreased. (Note that the full update rules are significantly more complicated than those presented here. See [96] for a more detailed description of the rules.)

To apply the HTM learning algorithm to a particular data source, Numenta uses optimization techniques to choose optional HTM components, select parameter values, and determine which data fields to include (http://youtube.com/watch?v=xYPKjKQ4YZ0).

## 11.6  Discussion and Summary

Classical AI solutions are task specific and brittle; they can only do one major thing and they fail too easily. Hawkins [27] and Numenta [96] have developed and implemented a general learning algorithm, the HTM learning algorithm, that overcomes the weaknesses of the classical solutions [108]. HTM's general learning rules are to train on every input; if a pattern is repeated, then reinforce it; and if a pattern is not repeated, then forget it.

When a new input vector arrives, it leads to a sparse set of active cell columns. One or more of the cells in each column become active; these cells, in turn, cause other cells to enter a predictive state through learned lateral connections between cells in different columns. The cells activated by the lateral connections constitute a prediction of what is likely to happen next. When the next input vector arrives, it selects another sparse set of active columns. If a newly active column is unexpected—meaning that it was not predicted by any cells—it will activate all the cells in the column. If a newly active column has one or more predicted cells, only those cells will become active. The output vector contains the feed-forward output of all cells.

While the current HTM realization has hundreds of millions of synapses (300 million using the numbers in this chapter), the brain has trillions of synapses, making it clear that the HTM implementation is only simulating a tiny part of the brain. In the future, it should be possible to connect HTMs together in hierarchies to obtain more brain-like simulations. At the time of this writing, Hawkins and Numenta are working to introduce motor control into HTM and refining the functionality according to the behavior of the cortex. In the next chapter, we consider how to use HTM to detect anomalies in cloud-based systems.

# Chapter 12
# Anomaly Detection with HTM

We model information and communications technology (ICT) systems as complex adaptive systems. Since we cannot hope to predict all future incidents in complex systems, real-time monitoring is needed to detect local failures before they propagate into global failures with an intolerable impact. In particular, monitoring is required to determine the consequences of injecting artificial errors into production systems and to learn how to avoid or limit the impact of future incidents.

In Part II we argued that anti-fragile ICT solutions in the cloud should have a service-oriented architecture with microservices, preferably created by development and operations (DevOps) teams. Since microservices depend on much fewer variables than a complete system, it is possible to monitor and diagnose microservice failures. However, the ability to monitor these services does not come for free [53]. DevOps teams need monitoring and logging setups for each type of microservice showing the up/down status, current throughput and latency, and details on circuit breaker status.

In this chapter, we discuss what an anomaly means and how the hierarchical temporal memory (HTM) learning algorithm detects anomalies in data streams. The HTM algorithm can be applied to many different types of data streams. Grok is an application that Numenta built on top of the Numenta Platform for Intelligent Computing (NuPIC) implementation of HTM (http://numenta.org/nupic.html) to detect anomalies in metric data provided by the Amazon Web Services (AWS) cloud. Here, we examine how Grok detects and displays anomalies in AWS streaming data. We then study how HTM detects rogue human behavior. The chapter is mostly based on information provided by Numenta [109, 110], including talks by Ahmad (http://youtube.com/watch?v=nVCKjZWYavM) and Purdy (http://youtube.com/watch?v=I5lSEHvngaI).

## 12.1 Anomalies

Complex ICT systems generate much data about their own operations. Cloud solutions are no exception. In fact, cloud providers offer services that allow solution owners to easily access operational data from their own cloud applications. The Internet

© The Author(s) 2016
K.J. Hole, *Anti-fragile ICT Systems*, Simula SpringerBriefs on Computing 1,
DOI 10.1007/978-3-319-30070-2_12

of Things will likely lead to a huge increase in sensors generating continuous data streams about the status of both natural and man-made systems. The many data streams from current and future systems will make it impossible to analyze all the data in detail. One interesting alternative is to look for anomalies in the streams to detect the beginning of failures. There is evidence that it is possible to detect the beginning of large failures in different types of complex adaptive systems before the impact becomes intolerable [111, 112].

Anomalies are data patterns that do not conform to expected behavior [113]. A data stream of patterns can have several types of anomalies. A *spatial* (static) *anomaly* is a single pattern or set of relatively closely spaced patterns in the data stream that deviates from what is standard, normal, or expected. A *temporal anomaly* is a set of surprising transitions between patterns. Note that it is the temporal sequence that is surprising, not the individual patterns themselves. If the patterns in a stream are highly random, then it is hard or even impossible to detect spatial and temporal anomalies. However, it is possible to detect a change in the distribution of the random data, denoted a *distribution anomaly*. All three types of anomalies are temporary anomalies. When a surprising change first appears, then it is an anomaly. If it appears multiple times, then it is the "new normal" and ceases to be an anomaly.

## 12.2  HTM Anomaly Score

The Grok application built on top of HTM detects spatial, temporal, and distribution anomalies. Since HTM is an online continuous learning system, it will detect temporary anomalies and quickly learn when they are the new normal. HTM works for both numerical and categorical input data. The two data types can be mixed in an input stream to HTM because they are both converted to a sparse distributed representation (SDR).

HTM calculates an *anomaly score* for each new pattern it receives [109]. If a received pattern was predicted, then the anomaly score is zero. If the pattern was not predicted at all, then the score is one. A partially predicted pattern has a score between zero and one. The actual score depends on the "similarity" between the actual received pattern and the predicted pattern. The similarity is determined by the SDR. The larger the overlap between actual and predicted bits in column space, the smaller the anomaly score.

If none of the cells in a column were predicted, then all the cells are made active. This process is referred to as *bursting*. It occurs when there is no context, that is, when HTM is learning a new transition. At each time instance, the anomaly score is simply the fraction given by the number of bursting columns divided by the total number of active columns. In the beginning of the training, the anomaly score will be high because most patterns will be new. As HTM learns, the anomaly score will diminish until there is a change in the pattern stream.

**Fig. 12.1** Normal
distribution of anomaly
scores divided into typical
values, somewhat
unexpected values, and
anomalies

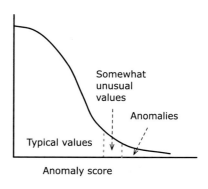

## 12.3  HTM Anomaly Probabilities

There are cases where the anomaly score is all that is needed to detect anomalies, but there are also cases where the anomaly score produces too many false positives because the metric data are very noisy. To deal with noise, we compute *anomaly probabilities*. The anomaly probability values are calculated relative to historical metric data rather than being absolute measurements of anomalous behavior. In other words, the goal is to detect changes in the anomaly score itself.

To determine anomaly probabilities, we consider a window of previous calculated anomaly scores and compute estimates of the expectation and standard deviation of the values, assuming normally distributed scores. Figure 12.1 depicts the right half of a normal distribution of possible score values. When a new anomaly score arrives, we estimate how likely the value is using the normal distribution based on the window of previous values. A new value on the $x$-axis under the central area of the curve in Fig. 12.1 is a typical value that we should expect to see often. Typical values of the anomaly score indicate that the system is operating as desired.

To detect anomalies, we look for values associated with the right tail of the computed normal distribution. Values falling in the beginning of the tail in Fig. 12.1 are somewhat unusual, while values further out in the tail represent anomalous behavior. Because the distribution of the anomaly scores can change over time, the estimates of the expectation and standard deviation of the normal distribution are recalculated as the window slides over the previously received scores.

## 12.4  Grok the Cloud

The word *grok* was coined by Robert A. Heinlein in his 1961 science fiction novel *Stranger in a Strange Land*. To grok means to understand so thoroughly that the observer becomes a part of the observed. Numenta has built an application called Grok on top of the NuPIC implementation of HTM to detect anomalies in metric data from the AWS cloud. The application utilizes HTM to learn streaming metrics

**Fig. 12.2** While the blue
curve showing CPU
utilization looks normal to
humans, Grok detected an
anomaly (picture from [109])

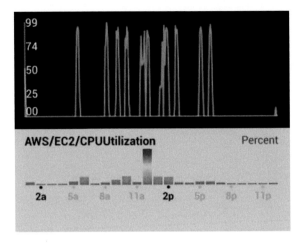

from virtual machine clusters and to identify anomalies in these metrics. Grok builds
a separate model for each monitored AWS metric. The metric values are combined
with timestamps to allow Grok to learn patterns related to the time of day or the
day of the week. To reduce the number of false positives, Grok calculates anomaly
probabilities.

Figure 12.2 shows a part of the Grok user interface. The blue graph with the black
background shows the CPU utilization of a virtual machine in the AWS cloud. The
corresponding anomaly score is shown directly below. Grok uses color-coded bars
to depict anomaly scores. The color and height of a bar have the same meaning,
making it easier to see anomalies. The three types of anomaly probabilities, typical,
somewhat unusual, and anomalies (see Fig. 12.1), are used to color the bars. Red
represents an anomaly, a highly improbable score with a probability around 0.001 %.
Yellow and green represent progressively more common scores.

The example in Fig. 12.2 illustrates that Grok can detect anomalies that are hard
for a human to see in a raw metric stream. When it is not obvious why Grok flagged
an anomaly, an operator can view the anomaly scores of other AWS metrics to gain
more insight. Since Grok builds an independent model for each monitored metric
stream, a system operator can obtain several independent confirmations that a virtual
machine has unusual behavior.

In the next example, a load balancer distributes requests from many clients over
a set of servers. The load balancer produces a fairly unpredictable or noisy metric stream showing the latency in serving web pages to clients. The blue curve in
Fig. 12.3 represents the metric values fed into Grok, while the green, yellow, and
red bars represent the anomaly scores colored according to the calculated anomaly
probabilities. The example illustrates that Grok can find anomalies in noisy data.

In Chap. 5, we discussed how software engineers induced artificial failures into
Netflix's media streaming system to discover vulnerabilities early, when their impacts
are small. Early vulnerability detection allows engineers to improve systems and

**Fig. 12.3** An anomalous
pattern detected within a
noisy metric stream from a
load balancer (picture from
[109])

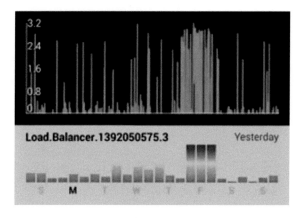

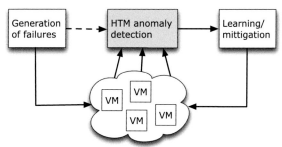

**Fig. 12.4** A process to
detect and mitigate the
impact of induced (and
natural) failures in virtual
machines (VMs)

avoid failures with intolerable impacts. The flow diagram in Fig. 12.4 illustrates how
Grok can be integrated into a process to detect and mitigate the impact of induced
(and natural) failures in applications running in the AWS cloud. How the learn-
ing/mitigation step will be carried out depends on the application being monitored.
Today, this step is carried out by humans. In the future, it may be possible to automate
at least part of the step.

## 12.5 Rogue Behavior

Numenta has developed an application for rogue behavior detection (RBD) based
on HTM [110]. Using human- and machine-generated data, the RBD application
automatically models an individual's behavior and identifies irregular actions. This
anomaly detection of irregular human behavior is useful for ICT security, device
access control, and fraud detection.

The RBD application has several attractive properties due to HTM. First, it is not
necessary to divide employees into classes and define what normal behavior is for
each class. Furthermore, there is no need for a separate training period or retraining,
since employee behavior changes over time. The application learns continuously in

**Fig. 12.5** An employee
anomaly (picture from [110])

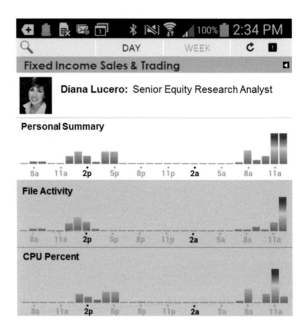

real time and builds a separate model for each monitored individual, thus achieving
high-precision anomaly detection for all individuals. The same high-quality detection
is generally not possible with class-based monitoring. Finally, real-time anomaly
detection enables quick corrective actions to avoid or at least reduce the negative
consequences of illegal actions.

Figure 12.5 shows part of the user interface for the RBD application. The senior
analyst monitored, Diana Lucero, is part of an experiment to test the application.
She exhibits unusual behavior at 11a.m. Drilling down to see the anomaly scores
for the individual metric streams, we find spikes in both the file activity and CPU
usage. Further investigation finds that the RBD application reacted because the analyst generated and stored a large .zip file containing intellectual property. The early
detection of this activity made it possible to stop the analyst from transmitting the
file to a third party.

## 12.6  Detecting the Beginning of Swans

In this book, we have assumed that there is no fundamental difference between
frequent incidents with a tolerable impact and rare incidents with an intolerable
impact, called swans. Most swans simply start out as local incidents that do not stop
but propagate due to positive feedback loops. According to Sect. 2.3, to predict any
future incident, we must describe the event, estimate its probability, and calculate
the impact. In Chap. 2, we argued that humans have limited ability to predict swans.

It is unlikely that a group of stakeholders will predict all potential swans in a complex adaptive ICT system, even if they use significant resources in classical risk analysis.

At the time of this writing, the detection of catastrophic events in real time is an active area of research [111, 112]. Because global or emergent failures very often start out as local failures in complex ICT systems, it is possible to detect the beginning of a swan in real time, even though we may not immediately understand the underlying reasons for its occurrence. HTM detects unlikely behavior by observing the fraction of bursting cell columns. Because HTM can be applied to different data streams, it can detect the beginning of swans in different types of complex ICT systems. It is still essential to realize the four design principles in Chap. 4 to avoid positive feedback loops that quickly propagate local failures into global failures before countermeasures can be introduced.

## 12.7   Discussion and Summary

Government agencies regulate many complex adaptive ICT systems of national importance. Unfortunately, it is very hard for a regulator to gain an adequate understanding of a complex ICT system without being closely involved in its design and daily operation. A regulator can set all kinds of non-functional requirements but cannot discover system fragilities or request useful improvements from afar. Regulation and compliance really only make sense for relatively simple systems that have one best method of working [18]. There will always be a significant gap between a regulator's understanding of a complex ICT system and the way it really operates. This gap must be filled by other stakeholders. This is particularly true for complex ICT systems with microservice architectures.

For a system to achieve anti-fragility to a class of negative events, stakeholders must monitor the operation of the microservices, especially their outputs, and detect anomalies. While information technology (IT) departments know how to monitor monolithic applications with single executables, it is more challenging to monitor applications of microservices running in clouds and communicating over network connections. Since a solution may fail even though all its microservices work according to their specifications (see Sect. 4.6), it may be necessary to trace the communication between services to understand why a particular service received input values for which it was not designed. Furthermore, there are many network connections where latency could cause intermediate problems. Hence, sophisticated monitoring of a large number of microservices and their communications is needed to detect anomalies, determine failures, and create anti-fragile solutions.

A comprehensive comparison of different techniques to detect anomalies in streaming data is outside the scope of this book. We have only illustrated how HTM detects anomalies in two domains. However, the performance results of Price [97], Galetzka [98], and Numenta [109, 110] strongly indicate that HTM is a good choice for anomaly detection in streaming data. In 2015, Numenta published source code and test data to compare the performance of anomaly detection algorithms. The initial results show that the HTM algorithm detects anomalies earlier than other popular algorithms (http://github.com/Numenta/NAB). If we have good anomaly detectors connected to a complex adaptive ICT system, then we can detect anomalies before the whole system breaks down. We have seen that HTM is able to detect changes before it is obvious to a human that a new problem is brewing.

A reader interested in more information about anomaly detection with HTM, as well as more examples detecting sudden, slow, and subtle anomalies, should study Numenta's two white papers [109, 110]. At the time of this writing, is also possible to use Grock for IT analytics and Grok for stocks on the Web.

---

**What to learn from Part IV**

Part IV introduced a novel learning algorithm based on Hawkins' HTM theory. HTM explains how the neocortex learns by modeling and processing data from the body's sensory organs. We concentrated on understanding how the HTM learning algorithm can detect anomalies in complex adaptive ICT systems. While most anomaly detection techniques are created to determine anomalies in data stored in databases, HTM finds anomalies in real-time streaming data. There is no need to store huge amounts of data since HTM builds models representing the properties of the data.

The ability to process streaming data makes the HTM learning algorithm ideal for applications running on cloud platforms since leading cloud providers offer services that stream metrics about an application's state. HTM's ability to process streaming data from a huge number of sensors also makes the algorithm perfect for monitoring the Internet of Things. While the current version of HTM is implemented in software, a hardware implementation is needed to seriously scale the algorithm's operation.

---

# Part V
# Future Anti-fragile Systems

# Chapter 13
# Summary and Future Work

We have come to the end of the book, which has investigated different aspects of anti-fragile information and communications technology (ICT) systems. Taleb [10] introduced the concept of anti-fragility to show that it is not enough for large natural or man-made systems to be robust to predictable events with a large impact. In an unpredictable world, systems must be able to handle randomness, volatility, and unforeseen large-impact events. Learning from artificial and real incidents is necessary to remove vulnerabilities and prevent systems from developing fragilities over time. This chapter summarizes the book's main insights into the development and operation of anti-fragile ICT systems, discusses the design of future systems, and outlines the need for anti-fragile processes, especially to handle attacks on the confidentiality, integrity, and availability of ICT systems.

## 13.1 Achieving Anti-fragility

While many commentators find Taleb's concept of anti-fragility both interesting and useful, other commentators believe it is very similar to the well-known concepts of robustness and resilience. To determine whether Taleb's work [10] really brings any new insight into the development and operation of large ICT systems, the author has investigated different aspects of anti-fragility. The main insights are summarized in the following.

Stakeholders of complex adaptive ICT systems must embrace hardware and software failures because they are inevitable. Local failures should, at worst, result in degraded performance, not systemic failures such as unplanned system downtime. The book introduced four design principles—*modularity*, *weak links*, *redundancy*, and *diversity*—to isolate the impact of local failures and one operational principle—the *fail fast* principle—to quickly detect vulnerabilities by inducing artificial failures. The collective goal of the five principles presented is to limit the impact of failures by failing early, isolate the impact of local failures, and learn from small

© The Author(s) 2016
K.J. Hole, *Anti-fragile ICT Systems*, Simula SpringerBriefs on Computing 1,
DOI 10.1007/978-3-319-30070-2_13

failures how to maintain the desired performance as a system and its environment change. Netflix's pioneering work shows that stakeholders can build and maintain web-scale applications in the cloud with a degree of anti-fragility to system downtime. Analyses of telecom infrastructures and electronic government systems confirm that the cloud facilitates anti-fragility to downtime.

A series of analyses outlined how to gain anti-fragility to the spreading of malware with unknown and time-varying spreading mechanisms. It was first found that application stores utilizing compilers with diversity engines in the cloud could generate enough software diversity to halt frequent malware outbreaks from spreading over huge networks of computing devices. Imperfect malware detection/removal was then added to this simple diversity-enhancing technique to keep the fraction of infected devices low over time. The resulting halting technique scales to prevent the spreading of frequent malware outbreaks on networks with millions of devices. While more work is needed to verify the practicability of the halting technique, the approach demonstrates that it is advantageous to model huge networked computing systems as complex adaptive systems and then apply results from network science to analyze the models' fragility, robustness, and anti-fragility to different classes of impacts.

If we cannot detect failures in a system, then it becomes impossible to determine and remove vulnerabilities. Hence, we must be able to monitor a system's behavior to ensure anti-fragility to a particular type of impact. We have argued that cloud-based software solutions should have a service-oriented architecture (SOA) with microservices implemented by virtual machines. While it is hard to monitor and analyze the internal behavior of applications with strongly connected modules, the simplicity of weakly connected microservices makes it possible to monitor and understand their individual behaviors. If the graph defining the dependencies between the microservices is not too large and dense, then it is also possible to analyze the consequences of the dependencies.

We need a technique to detect anomalies in streaming data because cloud infrastructures typically stream metric data about the status of virtual machines. Hawkins' learning algorithm is an interesting choice for anomaly detection in streaming data. The algorithm is based on a theory of how the brain learns, called hierarchical temporal memory (HTM). While the HTM learning algorithm may not always provide the best anomaly detection, it is very flexible and can be applied to many different metric streams. HTM automatically builds online data models, removing the need to store huge amounts of data in a database. Since the HTM algorithm is able to quickly detect anomalies, it facilitates corrective actions in real time. An application called Grok utilizes the HTM learning algorithm to detect anomalies in virtual machines running on the Amazon Web Services (AWS) cloud. Grok is able to detect anomalies that are hard for humans to see in the raw feed of AWS metric data. The application has also been successfully applied to user-defined metric streams.

In conclusion, many of today's ICT systems with strongly connected modules are too fragile to downtime and other large-impact events. While anti-fragile ICT systems have no absolute guarantee of avoiding the intolerable impact of all possible swan events, it is practicable to build systems that handle the impact of surprising events much better than many current systems. In a world where people are becoming increasingly dependent on ICT, we need to build anti-fragile systems to avoid rare but hugely negative events affecting whole populations.

## 13.2 Future Anti-fragile ICT Systems

Only complex adaptive ICT systems need to be anti-fragile to different classes of impacts because only complex systems are vulnerable to swans in the form of highly surprising, global failures with intolerable impact. We have concentrated on how to create anti-fragile systems in the cloud because its pay-as-you-go pricing model makes it economically feasible for even startups and other small companies to build anti-fragile solutions. Further investigation into the anti-fragility of ICT systems should consider whether additional design and operational principles, as well as anti-principles, are needed to ensure anti-fragility to different classes of impacts. A new principle should only be introduced if it is valid for many types of systems. The introduction of highly overlapping principles should be avoided.

Simplicity is an obvious candidate to become a general design principle for anti-fragile systems. We have already promoted simplicity by recommending the use of SOA with microservices. The single purpose of a microservice makes it easy to understand what each part of a system does. Furthermore, weak links between the services limits the effect of local failures and makes it easier to understand a system's overall behavior. However, more work is needed to understand the full meaning and impact of simplicity in the context of anti-fragile systems. New architectural patterns facilitating anti-fragility to classes of incidents would be particularly welcome. We also need to better understand the effort required to monitor anti-fragile systems.

Another obvious candidate to become a design principle is openness. Indirectly, we have also promoted openness by considering the anti-principle of closedness. Openness can undoubtedly reduce the negative impact of coincidental events. The advantage of openness is less clear when, for example, nation states are attacking each other's vital ICT infrastructures. More work is needed to fully understand the implications of openness in the context of anti-fragile systems of critical national or international importance.

The study of real systems is necessary to gain more insight into the concept of anti-fragility. While it is hard for independent scientists to obtain information on electronic payment systems, studies of such systems are of particular interest because of their great importance to society. It is particularly interesting to better understand how fraud detection can be exploited to achieve a degree of anti-fragility to financial losses.

The HTM theory discussed outlines how a small part of the neocortex learns sequences and predicts future inputs. While we applied HTM to detect anomalies in streaming metric data from the cloud, HTM theory has wider applications. The neocortex itself is an anti-fragile system (or system of systems) because it continuously learns new sequences and forgets old sequences in a way that is highly tolerant to noise, damaged cells, and broken connections. Future HTM theory is likely to provide important insights into the development of anti-fragile machine learning systems.

## 13.3   Future Bio-inspired System Designs

While superficial comparisons between complex adaptive ICT systems and biological systems should be avoided, it is useful to view distributed ICT systems as ecosystems or communities of autonomous entities interacting with each other and a changing environment. To encourage the reader to consider bio-inspired system designs in the future, we argue that ICT systems of simple and weakly connected modules avoid much of the fragility associated with strongly connected legacy systems based on old technologies that are hard to maintain and upgrade.

It is impossible to change an ICT system in a controlled manner if we do not understand its functionality. While a large ICT system has very diverse functionality, humans can only focus on one task at the time. When the human mind is forced to focus on multiple difficult tasks simultaneously, it tries to switch between tasks in rapid succession, making the effort of completing the tasks much more difficult. In particular, it is hard for software developers to understand the functionality of an ICT system consisting of many large, complicated software modules. As the original developers of a software system move to other projects and new developers start to modify the original code, the initial design is often violated. Many of these design violations occur unintentionally because the new developers do not fully understand the original system design and its implementation. Over time, the many changes to the original code generate more and stronger dependencies between the modules, resulting in a strongly connected system that is vulnerable to failure propagation causing systemic failures.

In general, the more tasks an engineer or developer has to consider at the same time to create some kind of module, the more complicated the module is. The development of simple modules, each with a single limited responsibility, helps explain why the class of microservice architectures first discussed in Chap. 5 is becoming increasingly popular. Since each microservice fulfills a single responsibility, one developer can understand the functionality of the microservice without undue strain. Furthermore, the developers in a team creating a microservice solution can concentrate on a single task at a time, making it more pleasurable to develop the solution.

The class of microservice architectures with weak links is the result of years of engineering work in building web-scale applications with very high availability, scalability, and performance. A microservice solution mimics nature. The whole system is constantly evolving, without the limited availability associated with monoliths. In particular, microservices come and go. Microservice solutions are "living software" that remove much of the fragility of legacy software because it is easy to remove old services and create new ones. In fact, developers often write a completely new microservice rather than modify an old service, because the limited functionality makes it easy to write a service from scratch.

Experience with microservice solutions suggests that building systems with simple and weakly connected modules can significantly reduce the fragility associated with legacy systems. The functionality of a system should be divided over many modules such that a single human can understand what each module does without undue effort. Weak links, redundancy, and diversity should then be used to limit the impact of local failures.

## 13.4  The Need for Anti-fragile Processes

While we have mainly considered how to design and implement anti-fragile ICT systems, another related approach to anti-fragility is to consider systems and their stakeholders as adaptive complex processes. This view provides us with a very general approach to the study of anti-fragility. In fact, a process may very well be anti-fragile to a particular type of undesirable outcome without any technology involved at all. Hence, we could study processes in the area of computer science, as well as society in general, to better understand fragility, robustness, and anti-fragility to particular impacts.

The international research community in cryptography has long deployed anti-fragile processes to develop new cryptographic solutions. A universally accepted cryptographic primitive such as a cipher or a hash function is the result of a competitive process in which some researchers suggest new primitives and other researchers try to determine if the primitives have exploitable vulnerabilities. After several rounds of modified suggestions and attacks, a new primitive emerges that is very hard to compromise because the cryptographers have learned from their own and others' earlier mistakes. However, even after this long and hard selection process, cryptographers know that the only way to ensure a primitive's strength over time is to keep attacking it on a regular basis. The same is true for cryptographic protocols.

One example of this never-ending anti-fragile process is the many evaluations of the Transport Layer Security (TLS) protocol, leading to new and more secure protocol versions. However, the serious Heartbleed Bug incident demonstrated that large-impact incidents can still occur. While many have evaluated the TLS design through the years and mitigated vulnerabilities, it is also necessary to carefully validate the implementations of TLS. The Heartbleed Bug disclosed in April 2014 involved an improper input validation in the OpenSSL cryptography library, a much used implementation of the TLS protocol. The missing bounds check allowed theft of the servers' private keys and users' session cookies and passwords. While many large companies used the OpenSSL cryptography library, it seems that none of them had carefully validated the code. This serious incident demonstrates the danger of trusting software libraries without evaluating the security of the code. Trust by default must be replaced by an understood degree of trust.

To improve the security of complex adaptive ICT systems, it is necessary to develop anti-fragile processes to maintain a high level of confidentiality, integrity, and availability. As argued in Chap. 2, risk management processes based on the prediction of incidents are not enough because the risk of a complex ICT system may very well be dominated by swans, which are notoriously difficult to predict. Hence, we need anti-fragile security processes that limit the impact of inevitable security incidents and learn from these incidents how to create more secure systems. Everybody with the ability to change the security of an ICT system should have "skin in the game," that is, they should share the responsibility for the consequences of a successful attack, not to be punished but to ensure a subsequent period of learning and mitigation to improve security and to stop similar attacks in the future.

## 13.5  Challenge to Readers

The author wrote this book to educate himself and the reader about anti-fragile ICT systems and to argue that it is both possible and desirable to develop and operate such systems. Some of the book's specific proposals will undoubtedly be replaced by better solutions, while others will hopefully survive. Since our knowledge of anti-fragile ICT systems is still limited and fragmented, more work is needed to better understand these systems. Improvements to the outlined solutions are very welcome, as well as brand new solutions with anti-fragility to different types of impacts. To model real systems, create anti-fragile processes, and discover ways to improve and extend the contents of the book, the interested reader will do well to first study the many surprising perspectives, interesting ideas, and important insights introduced by Taleb [8–12], Dekker [17, 18], and Geer [28–33].

# References

1. D.H. Meadows, *Thinking in Systems: A Primer*, Chelsea Green Publishing, 2008.
2. J.P. Crutchfield, "The Hidden Fragility of Complex Systems—Consequences of Change, Changing Consequences," in *Cultures of Change: Social Atoms and Electronic Lives*, edited by G. Ascione, C. Massip, and J. Perello, Actard Publishers, 2009, pp. 98–111.
3. D. Helbing, "Systemic Risks in Society and Economics," SFI Working Paper 2009-12-044, 2009, www.santafe.edu/media/workingpapers/09-12-044.pdf.
4. D. Helbing, "Globally Networked Risks and How to Respond," *Nature*, vol. 497, 2013, pp. 51–59.
5. S.M. Rinaldi, J.P. Peerenboom, and T.K. Kelly, "Identifying, Understanding, and Analyzing Critical Infrastructure Interdependencies," *IEEE Control Systems*, vol. 21, no. 6, 2001, pp. 11–25.
6. R.G. Little, "Controlling Cascading Failure: Understanding the Vulnerabilities of Interconnected Infrastructures," *Journal of Urban Technology*, vol. 9, no. 1, 2002, pp. 109–123.
7. K.J. Hole, "Management of Hidden Risks," *IEEE Computer*, vol. 46, no. 1, 2013, pp. 65–70.
8. N.N. Taleb, *Fooled by Randomness: The Hidden Role of Chance in Life and in the Markets*, 2nd edition, Random House, 2005.
9. N.N. Taleb, *The Black Swan: The Impact of the Highly Improbable*, 1st edition, Random House, 2007. See also the 2nd edition from 2010 with a new essay on robustness and fragility.
10. N.N. Taleb, *Antifragile: Things That Gain from Disorder*, Random House, 2012.
11. N.N. Taleb, "The Fourth Quadrant: A Map of the Limits of Statistics," Edge, 14 September 2008.
12. N.N. Taleb, R. Read, R. Douady, J. Norman, and Y. Bar-Yam, "The Precautionary Principle (with Application to the Genetic Modification of Organisms)," 2014, arxiv.org/abs/1410.5787.
13. M.J. Kavis, *Architecting the Cloud*, Wiley, 2014.
14. B. Wilder, *Cloud Architecture Patterns*, O'Reilly, 2012.
15. C. Perrow, *Normal Accidents: Living with High-Risk Technologies*, Princeton University Press, 1999.
16. J.H. Miller and S.E. Page, *Complex Adaptive Systems*, Princeton University Press, 2007.
17. S. Dekker, *Drift into Failure*, Ashgate, 2011.
18. S. Dekker, *Safety Differently*, 2nd edition, CRC Press, 2014.
19. S. Robinson and M.M. Robinson, *Holonomics*, Floris Books, 2014.
20. C. Gros, *Complex and Adaptive Dynamical Systems*, Springer, 2008.
21. C.C. Elisan, *Malware, Rootkits & Botnets*, McGraw-Hill Osborne Media, 2012.
22. Q. Li and G. Clark, "Mobile Security: A Look Ahead," *Security & Privacy*, vol. 11, no. 1, 2013, pp. 78–81.
23. M.E.J. Newman, *Networks: An Introduction*, Oxford University Press, 2010.

© The Author(s) 2016

K.J. Hole, *Anti-fragile ICT Systems*, Simula SpringerBriefs on Computing 1,
DOI 10.1007/978-3-319-30070-2

24. M. Franz, "E Unibus Pluram: Massive-Scale Software Diversity as a Defense Mechanism," *Proceedings of the New Security Paradigms Workshop 2010*, Concord, MA, 21–23 September 2010, pp. 7–16.

25. R. Cohen, S. Havlin, and D. Ben-Avraham, "Efficient Immunization Strategies for Computer Networks and Populations," *Physical Review Letters*, vol. 91, no. 24, Article ID 247901, 2003.

26. D. Montague, *Essentials of Online Payment Security and Fraud Prevention*, Wiley, 2011.

27. J. Hawkins and S. Blakeslee, *On Intelligence*, Times Books, 2004.

28. D.E. Geer, "Monopoly Considered Harmful," *IEEE Security & Privacy*, vol. 1, no. 6, 2003, pp. 14–17.

29. D.E. Geer, "Monoculture on the Back of the Envelope," *;login:*, vol. 30, no. 6, 2005, pp. 6–8.

30. D.E. Geer, "Dan Geer Keynote," Source 2008 Conference, Boston, MA, 13 March 2008, http://geer.tinho.net/geer.sourceboston.txt.

31. D.E. Geer, "Dan Geer Keynote," Source 2012 Conference, Boston, MA, 18 April 2012, http://geer.tinho.net/geer.sourceboston.18iv12.txt.

32. D.E. Geer, "Complexity Is the Enemy," *IEEE Security & Privacy*, vol. 6, no. 6, 2008, p. 88.

33. D. E. Geer, "People in the Loop: Are They a Failsafe or a Liability?" Suits & Spooks, 8 February 2012, http://tinyurl.com/7cavobr.

34. K.J. Hole and L.-H. Netland, "Toward Risk Assessment of Large-Impact and Rare Events," *IEEE Security & Privacy*, vol. 8, no. 3, 2010, pp. 21–27.

35. M.T. Nygard, *Release It!* Pragmatic Bookshelf, 2007.

36. D. Kahneman, *Thinking, Fast and Slow*, Farrar, Straus and Giroux, 2011.

37. J. Humble, J. Molesky, and B. O'Reilly, *Lean Enterprise*, O'Reilly Media, 2015.

38. D. Zwieback, "Antifragile Systems and Teams," O'Reilly Media, 2014.

39. P. Triana, *Lecturing Birds on Flying: Can Mathematical Theories Destroy the Financial Markets?* Wiley, 2009.

40. B. Mandelbrot and R.L. Hudson, *The (Mis)behavior of Markets: A Fractal View of Financial Turbulence*, annotated edition, Basic Books, 2006.

41. A. Tseitlin, "The Antifragile Organization," *Communications of the ACM*, vol. 56, no. 8, 2013, pp. 40–44.

42. S.C. Currall and M.J. Epstein, "The Fragility of Organizational Trust: Lessons From the Rise and Fall of Enron," *Organizational Dynamics*, vol. 32, no. 2, 2003, pp. 193–206.

43. L.H. Nestås and K.J. Hole, "Building and Maintaining Trust in Internet Voting," *IEEE Computer*, vol. 45, no. 5, 2012, pp. 74–80.

44. E.A. Whitley and G. Hosein, *Global Challenges for Identity Policies*, Palgrave Macmillan, 2010.

45. E. Pieri, "ID Cards: A Snapshot of the Debate in the UK Press," project report, ESRC National Centre for e-Social Science, University of Manchester, 2009.

46. U. Wilensky, NetLogo, Center for Connected Learning and Computer-Based Modeling, Northwestern University, Evanston, IL, 1999, https://ccl.northwestern.edu/netlogo.

47. G.S. Lynch, *Single Point of Failure*, Wiley, 2009.

48. L. Bass, P. Clements, and R. Kazman, *Software Architecture in Practice*, 3rd edition, Addison-Wesley, 2012.

49. P. Csermely, *Weak Links*, Springer, 2006.

50. S.E. Page, *Diversity and Complexity*, Princeton University Press, 2010.

51. Y. Bar-Yam, "The Limits of Phenomenology: From Behaviourism to Drug Testing and Engineering Design," New England Complex Systems Institute (NECSI) Report 2013-08-01, arxiv.org/abs/1308.3094.

52. M. Richards, *Software Architecture Patterns*, O'Reilly Media, 2015.

53. S. Newman, *Building Microservices*, O'Reilly Media, 2015.

54. L. Krause, *Microservices: Patterns and Applications*, Amazon Digital Services, 2015.

55. P.J. Sadalage and M. Fowler, *NoSQL Distilled: A Brief Guide to the Emerging World of Polyglot Persistence*, Addison-Wesley, 2012.

56. K.J. Hole, "Diversity Reduces the Impact of Malware," *IEEE Security & Privacy*, vol. 13, no. 3, 2015, pp. 48–54.

57. Det Norske Veritas, "Vurdering av Altinn II-platformen," report in Norwegian commissioned by the Norwegian Ministry of Trade and Industry, version 1.1, 2012.
58. Capgemini Norge, "Altinn—en plattform å satse på?" report in Norwegian commissioned by the Norwegian Ministry of Trade and Industry, 2012.
59. Ministry of Government Administration, Reform and Church Affairs, "Digitizing Public Sector Services," Norwegian eGovernment Program, 2012, https://www.regjeringen.no/en/dokumenter/digitization-public-sector-services/id698435.
60. Government ministers Karl Eirik Schjøtt-Pedersen and Rigmor Aasrud discussed the effort to digitalize Norway's public sector, Digitaliseringskonferansen, Oslo, Norway, 30–31 May 2012.
61. Video by The Guardian, "How Geeks Opened up Government," 2013, www.guardian.co.uk/technology/video/2013/jun/13/geeks-opened-up-government-video.
62. K.J. Hole, "Building Trust in E-Government Services," *IEEE Computer*, vol. 49, no. 1, 2016, pp. 66–74.
63. P. Rost, C.J. Bernardos, A. De Domenico, M. Di Girolamo, M. Lalam, A. Maeder, D. Sabella, and D. Wübben, "Cloud Technologies for Flexible 5G Radio Access Networks," *IEEE Communications Magazine*, vol. 52, no. 5, 2014, pp. 68–76.
64. M.S. Dayananda and J. Priyanka, "Managing Software Defined Radio through Cloud Computing," *Proceedings of the IEEE International Conference on Advanced Communication Control and Computing Technologies*, Ramanathapuram, India, 23–25 August 2012, pp. 50–55.
65. I.R. Lorange, "Hendelsesrapport: Problemer i Telenors mobilnett 10. juni 2011," report from Telenor in Norwegian.
66. Post- og teletilsynet, "Hendelsesrapport: Utfall i Telenors mobilnett 10. juni 2011," report from the Norwegian Post and Telecommunications Authority in Norwegian.
67. I.R. Lorange, "Hendelsesrapport: Problemer i Telenors mobilnett 17. juni 2011," report from Telenor in Norwegian.
68. Post- og teletilsynet, "Hendelsesrapport om utfall i Telenors mobilnett 17. juni 2011," report from the Norwegian Post and Telecommunications Authority in Norwegian.
69. R. Dyrlie, "Hendelsesrapport 2: Problemer i Telenors mobilnett 10. juni 2011," report from Telenor in Norwegian.
70. Post- og teletilsynet, "Foreløpige erfaringer og forslag til tiltak etter ekstremværet Dagmar," report from the Norwegian Post and Telecommunications Authority in Norwegian, 2012.
71. Direktoratet for samfunnssikkerhet og beredskap, "Teknologiskiftet i Telenors infrastruktur," report from the Norwegian Directorate for Civil Protection in Norwegian, 2013.
72. K.J. Hole, O. Lysne, and S. Maharjan, "Consequences of the Trust Relationship between Telecom Operators and Vendors," white paper from Simula Research Laboratory, version 0.9.2, 2014.
73. Post- og teletilsynet, "Hendelsesrapport: Dobbelt fiberbrudd i Telenors nett, 23. mai 2011," report from the Norwegian Post and Telecommunications Authority in Norwegian.
74. "Kost-/nyttevurdering av tiltak for styrking av norsk sambands- og IP-infrastruktur," risk analysis in Norwegian by Nexia and Styrmand for the Norwegian Post and Telecommunications Authority.
75. B. Potter, "Necessary but Not Sufficient," *IEEE Security & Privacy*, vol. 8, no. 5, 2010, pp. 57–58.
76. E.M. Hutchins, M.J. Cloppert, and R.M. Amin, "Intelligence-Driven Computer Network Defense Informed by Analysis of Adversary Campaigns and Intrusion Kill Chains," *Proceedings of the Sixth International Conference on Information Warfare and Security*, Washington, DC, 17–18 March 2011, pp. 113–125.
77. P. Larsen, A. Homescu, S. Brunthaler, and M. Franz, "SoK: Automated Software Diversity," *Proceedings of the 35th IEEE Symposium on Security and Privacy*, San Jose, CA, 18–21 May 2014, pp. 276–291.
78. M. Garcia, A. Bessani, I. Gashi, N. Neves, and R. Obelheiro, "OS Diversity for Intrusion Tolerance: Myth or Reality?" *Proceedings of the 2011 IEEE/IFIP 41st International Conference on Dependable Systems & Networks*, Washington, DC, 27–30 June 2011, pp. 383–394.

79. J. Han, D. Gao, and R.H. Deng, "On the Effectiveness of Software Diversity: A Systematic Study on Real-World Vulnerabilities," *Proceedings of the Sixth International Conference on Detection of Intrusions and Malware, and Vulnerability Assessment*, Milan, Italy, 9–10 July 2009, pp. 127–146.

80. J. Balthrop, S. Forrest, M.E.J. Newman, and M.M. Williamson, "Technological Networks and the Spread of Computer Viruses," *Science*, vol. 304, no. 5670, 2004, pp. 527–529.

81. M. Kitsak, L.K. Gallos, S. Havlin, F. Liljeros, L. Muchnik, H.E. Stanley, and H.A. Makse, "Identification of Influential Spreaders in Complex Networks," *Nature Physics*, vol. 6, no. 11, 2010, pp. 888–893.

82. K.J. Hole, "Toward a Practical Technique to Halt Multiple Virus Outbreaks on Computer Networks," *Journal of Computer Networks and Communications*, vol. 2012, Article ID 462747, December 2012, http://www.hindawi.com/journals/jcnc/2012/462747/.

83. T. Jackson, B. Salamat, A. Homescu, K. Manivannan, G. Wagner, A. Gal, S. Brunthaler, Ch. Wimmer, and M. Franz, "Compiler-Generated Software Diversity," in *Moving Target Defense: Creating Asymmetric Uncertainty for Cyber Threats*, edited by S. Jajodia, A.K. Ghosh, V. Swarup, C. Wang, and X.S. Wang, Springer, 2011, pp. 77–98.

84. K. Kravvaritis, D. Mitropoulos, and D. Spinellis, "Cyberdiversity: Measures and Initial Results," *Proceedings of the 14th Panhellenic Conference on Informatics*, Tripoli, Greece, 10–12 September 2010, pp. 135–140.

85. P. Wang, M.C. González, C.A. Hidalgo, and A.-L. Barabási, "Understanding the Spreading Patterns of Mobile Phone Viruses," *Science*, vol. 324, no. 5930, 2009, pp. 1071–1076.

86. J. Caballero, T. Kampouris, D. Song, and J. Wang, "Would Diversity Really Increase the Robustness of the Routing Infrastructure against Software Defects?" Technical Report CMU-Cylab-07-002, Department of Electrical and Computer Engineering, Carnegie Mellon University, 2008, http://repository.cmu.edu/ece/40/.

87. J.O. Kephart and S.R. White, "Directed-Graph Epidemiological Models of Computer Viruses," *Proceedings of the 1991 IEEE Computer Society Symposium on Research in Security and Privacy*, Oakland, CA, May, 1991, pp. 343–359.

88. J. Maeda, *The Laws of Simplicity*, MIT Press, 2006.

89. P. Larsen, S. Brunthaler, and M. Franz, "Security through Diversity: Are We There Yet?" *IEEE Security & Privacy*, vol. 12, no. 2, 2014, pp. 28–35.

90. K.J. Hole, "Towards Anti-fragility: A Malware-Halting Technique," *IEEE Security & Privacy*, vol. 13, no. 4, 2015, pp. 40–46.

91. K. Salah, J.M. Alcaraz Calero, S. Zeadally, S. Al-Mulla, and M. Alzaabi, "Using Cloud Computing to Implement a Security Overlay Network," *Security & Privacy*, vol. 11, no. 1, 2013, pp. 44–53.

92. E.G. Amoroso, "From the Enterprise Perimeter to a Mobility-Enabled Secure Cloud," *Security & Privacy*, vol. 11, no. 1, 2013, pp. 23–31.

93. M. Abadi, M. Budiu, Ú. Erlingsson, and J. Ligatti, "Control-Flow Integrity Principles, Implementations, and Applications," *ACM Transactions on Information and System Security*, vol. 13, no. 1, 2009.

94. J. Milliken, V. Selis, and A. Marshall, "Detection and Analysis of the Chameleon WiFi Access Point Virus," *EURASIP Journal on Information Security*, vol. 2013, no. 2, 2013.

95. A.-L. Barabási, R. Albert, and H. Jeong, "Scale-Free Characteristics of Random Networks: The Topology of the World-Wide Web," *Physica A*, vol. 281, no. 1–4, 2000, pp. 69–77.

96. Numenta, "Hierarchical Temporal Memory," white paper, version 0.2.1, 2011.

97. R.W. Price, "Hierarchical Temporal Memory Cortical Learning Algorithm for Pattern Recognition on Multi-core Architectures," Master's Thesis, Portland State University, 2011.

98. M. Galetzka, "Intelligent Predictions: An Empirical Study of the Cortical Learning Algorithm," Master's Thesis, Department of Computer Science, University of Applied Sciences Mannheim, 2014.

99. J. Hertz, A. Krogh, and R.G. Palmer, *Introduction to the Theory of Neural Computation*, Addison-Wesley, 1991.

100. J.H. Holland, *Adaption in Natural and Artificial Systems*, MIT Press, 1992.

101. J. Copeland, *Artificial Intelligence: A Philosophical Introduction*, Wiley-Blackwell, 1993.
102. Y. LeCun, Y. Bengio, and G. Hinton, "Deep Learning," *Nature*, vol. 521, 2015, pp. 436–444.
103. J. Fodor, *The Mind Doesn't Work That Way*, MIT Press, 2000.
104. R. Penrose, *The Emperor's New Mind: Concerning Computers, Minds, and the Laws of Physics*, Oxford University Press, 1989.
105. R. Penrose, *Shadows of the Mind: A Search for the Missing Science of Consciousness*, Oxford University Press, 1994.
106. D.J. Chalmers, *The Conscious Mind*, Oxford University Press, 1996.
107. V.B. Mountcastle, "An Organizing Principle for Cerebral Function: The Unit Model and the Distributed System," in *The Mindful Brain*, edited by G.M. Edelman and V.V. Mountcastle, MIT Press, 1978, pp. 7–50.
108. S. Ahmad and J. Hawkins, "Properties of Sparse Distributed Representations and their Application to Hierarchical Temporal Memory," 2015, arxiv.org/abs/1503.07469.
109. Numenta, "The Science of Anomaly Detection," white paper, 2014.
110. Numenta, "Rogue Behavior Detection," white paper, 2014.
111. M. Scheffer, J. Bascompte, W.A. Brock, V. Brovkin, S.R. Carpenter, V. Dakos, H. Held, E.H. van Nes, M. Rietkerk, and G. Sugihara, "Early-Warning Signals for Critical Transitions," *Nature*, vol. 461, 2009, pp. 53–59.
112. D. Sornette, "Dragon-Kings, Black Swans and the Prediction of Crises," 2009, arxiv.org/abs/0907.4290.
113. V. Chandola, A. Banerjee, and V. Kumar, "Anomaly Detection: A Survey," *ACM Computing Surveys*, vol. 41, no. 3, article no. 15, 2009.

# Index

© The Author(s) 2016
K.J. Hole, *Anti-fragile ICT Systems*, Simula SpringerBriefs on Computing 1,
DOI 10.1007/978-3-319-30070-2

Printed in the United States
By Bookmasters